D1205696

A HISTORY OF ART
RENOIR
THE GREAT MASTERS

Pages 1, 3, 7, 9: Donald Lilly (design),
Jerry McFarland (photography)
Page 170: Frederic Jochem (design),
John Hall (photography).

Distributed worldwide by Baker + Taylor International
652 East Main Street, Bridgewater, New Jersey 08807
(908) 218-0400. Fax: (908) 707-4387

Published by Barons Who's Who
412 North Coast Highway, B-110, Laguna Beach, California 92651
(714) 497-8615. Fax: (714) 786-8918
http://baronswhoswho.com

10 9 8 7 6 5 4 3 2 1

Library of Congress Catalogue Number 97-061088
International Standard Book Number 1-882292-08-1

Typography by Typesetting & Graphics, Foothill Ranch, California
Printed and bound in Singapore

GREAT DESIGNERS OF THE WORLD

John L. Pellam

with Corinne Z. Kopen

Foreword by Donald Lilly, ASID

BARONS WHO'S WHO

TABLE OF CONTENTS

FOREWORD

You are about to embark on a visual journey that will take you into some of the most luxurious interiors in the world with projects spanning the globe, from North and South America, Asia, Europe, the Caribbean and the Middle East.

The following pages highlight the works of some of the most talented and innovative interior designers in the world. Each a visionary in their own right, and each driven by a passion that fuels their imagination and creativity.

The selection of an interior designer is a highly personalized one. The place where we live, work, spend time with family and friends, and relax should be an expression of your personality highlighted by the talents of your interior designer. Therefore, compatibility is essential. Designers must have the ability to assess your lifestyle, assimilate your needs and interests, appreciate and respect your concerns, while introducing you to new directions and creative ideas. In addition, designers must have the ability to work within a broad range of styles and parameters, from classic traditional to ultra contemporary settings, from grand scale residential to corporate headquarters. Great design is not only about furnishings and fabrics, but the integration of proper scale and balance, functionality and practicality. Attention to detail is crucial; a careful study of all aspects of the given space must be made prior to any actual planning. The final design, while always considering the aesthetic, must primarily address the functional use of the space in conjunction with any budgetary and scheduling constraints.

With the computer age upon us, rapid advancement modern technology, including the internet, e-mail, auto cad and fax machines, has enabled designers to successfully complete long distance projects, not only in their state or country, but worldwide – bringing their talents directly to your doorstep.

While perusing the following pages, consider that your dream can become a reality in the able hands of one of the following 'Great Designers of the World'.

– Donald W. Lilly, ASID

❦

"It is quite impossible to consider the building one thing and its
furnishings another, its setting and environs still another.
In the spirit in which buildings are conceived, these are all one thing
to be foreseen and provided for in the nature of the structure."

– Frank Lloyd Wright, 1909

INTRODUCTION

Great design, both architectural and interior, can be created by only a particularly talented few. *Great Designers of the World* captures the essence of great design in photographic form, and presents you with colorful images of spectacular design achievements from throughout the world.

But what makes a designer or architect truly great? Many elements are involved in creating world-class design: historical knowledge, for example, is as critical to realizing the French Provincial dreams a client may have for a high-rise apartment as it is to the accurate restoration of a colonial farmhouse. Although the general goal is timelessness, great designers have a detailed understanding of trends past, present, and even future. As with the other arts, design is subject to changing schools of discipline, as can be witnessed by the recent waves of deconstruction and post-modernism. Economic expertise is crucial to the successful negotiation of subcontracts as well as to sparing a client undue financial anguish.

The skills of today's great designers go far beyond the requirements of the professionals of even five years ago. If the above disciplines are necessary to creating great designs in the modern world, so are flexibility, speed and a calm demeanor in the face of disaster. Creating lasting beauty with a variety of materials in a disposable society is an artform in and of itself.

The stress created in today's age of technology and the increasing demand for instant information have created an equally increasing demand for serene areas for both living and working. Great design today requires the creation of spaces that are nurturing, reassuring, practical, efficacious, comfortable and restful. The realization of these spaces is the task of the design professional, a person who understands and anticipates our needs, such that he or she must practically become an extension of our own tastes, needs and lifestyles. The argot of the profession may be arcane, including such forbidding terms as *passementerie, chinoiserie* and *trompe l'oeil,* but the goal is relatively simple (in explanation, if not execution): to create an enduring environment that expresses, stretches, complements and pleases the client. And our goal is to offer those environments to you here in published form.

Great Designers of the World will also keep you apprised of the next design trends, since all of these artists are, to use a current phrase, 'on the cutting edge'. New trends are born of new inventions, events and discoveries. But it is the genius of the great designer that turns the new into the timeless, the trendy into the classic; and it is the genius of the great designer that has created the images which are presented to you upon the following pages of this volume.

– John L. Pellam

ADAMS DESIGN, INC.

Honolulu, Hawaii

Jack Adams earned his Bachelor's degree from West Point, a Bachelor of Arts degree from the Art Center College of Design, and has done postgraduate work at a number of other schools and universities. He was a project designer for Richard Crowell & Associates for three years, and then worked as a director of interior design for Media 5 Architects before becoming interior designer and marketing director for Dale Keller & Associates. Mr. Adams is currently president and principal designer of Adams Design, Inc., which he established in 1977. Jack is a Professional Member of the American Society of Interior Designers, and his work has been featured in numerous design-related publications, most recently in *Island Home Magazine*.

His philosophy stresses that a designer must interpret the client's innermost feelings of image, whether the client is individual or corporate, and this requires continuous attention from concept to completion. He feels that one of the main strengths of Adams Design is the sense of place and heritage they are able to convey in their design work. To quote, "Our hotel design conveys the warmth of a residence. Our residential design captures the drama usually seen only in hotel design." Adams Design is big enough to handle production on a timely basis, but small enough for the principal designer to give each client his personal attention.

"This entertainment lounge is inspired by the architecture and fresco art of the Etruscans. The custom columns are unique to this era and are multiplied into carefully placed mirrored walls, giving an illusion of a colonade. The pool room features a dome ceiling painting of antiquity and a waiting area that is reminiscent of an arabesque scene from *Tales of 1,000 and One Nights.*"

To contact Jack Adams, call (808) 955-6100 or fax (808) 947-4311; Jack's office is located at 1415 Kalakaua Avenue, Suite 204, Honolulu, Hawaii 96826.

AHARA PRIMA DESIGN PT

Kuningan, Jakarta, Indonesia

Gaby Widajanti graduated with honors from Germany's Technishe University in 1977 after studying Architecture at the University of Tarumanegara, Jakarta, Indonesia. Working with Bent Severin Consultant in Singapore gave her valuable experience in design coordination, office management, marketing and presentation. She used that experience to establish her own firm, the Ahara Prima Design PT in Jakarta. Ms. Widajanti is a Professional Member of the Indonesian Designer Association.

"This corporate office for Conbloc Indonesia PT is located in Jakarta, where the Board of Directors holds corporate and casual meetings. The entrance is designed to be private to the staff inside, while also giving visitors a glimpse of the conference room and city skyline. Two wooden columns pose a gateway, separated by different floorings of sandstone and carpet, to the central core of offices. The view of the city is unobstructed by using full glass partitions and doors to the perimeter offices.

"I chose the local timber of *meranti* for a traditional feeling, and used fabrics and artwork to maintain a modern appearance. Asian elements of *feng shui* were incorporated for harmony and balance. A free flow of *chi* to suit the chairman of the corporation was essential."

To contact Gaby Widajanti, call (62) 21-526-1370 or fax (62) 21-526-1470; Gaby's office is located at Graha Irama Building, Suite 8-D, Jalan H.R. Rasuna Said, Block X-1, Kav. 1-2, Kuningan, Jakarta 12950, Indonesia.

PHOTOGRAPHY: IWAN WINARNO

RASHID SAAD AL-RASHID

Riyadh, Saudi Arabia

Architect Rashid S. Al-Rashid was born in the Al-Hasa Oasis, located on the eastern province of the Kingdom of Saudi Arabia. Rashid was educated in the United States where he received his degree in Architecture from the University of Oregon. He then returned to his homeland of Saudi Arabia and established his own architectural firm in 1975 in Riyadh, where he served as principal architect. In 1976, Interior Architect Othman Al-Sulaiman joined him, and together they formed the Architectural Center for Design and Consultation.

"Throughout my twenty-four years of experience in the designing of community houses, palaces, residential complexes, mosques and shopping malls, I thought it was time for me to give an expressive gift to my lovely wife and to my five beautiful children who stood beside me throughout the hard times. This gift is a farmhouse in my hometown Al-Hasa Oasis, situated amongst more than two million date palm trees and a lime orchard. I have been attracted and influenced by an environmental design such as that applied in the Middle East and Santa Fe, New Mexico. I appreciate the careful use of that region's building materials – the wood, clay tiles, and soft colors. It was a challenge for me to integrate the concept of privacy into the large reception areas, which accommodate more than one hundred guests. I wanted to design this farmhouse to reflect my unique style of architectural design.

"I carefully studied the surrounding environment, including temperature, direction of the sun, orientation, and color scheme. The building, terraces and swimming pool blend together to form a welcoming resort surrounded by date palms, the lime orchard and assorted greenery. My wife played a big role in choosing the color scheme of the walls inside the house. Today, we look forward to spending our weekends there whether entertaining or relishing our privacy."

To contact Rashid Al-Rashid, please call him at (966) 1-403-0521; Rashid's office is located at Al-Rashid Center, Post Office Box 16557, Riyadh 11474, Saudi Arabia. Contractor: R.T.C.C., Post Office Box 307, Riyadh 11411, Saudi Arabia. Construction Manager: Eng. Marwane Nasrah.

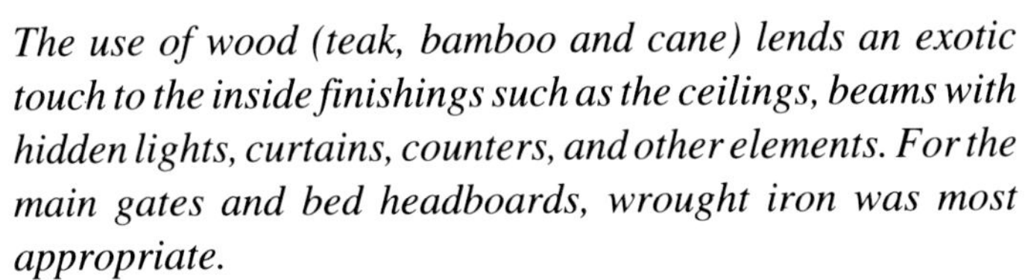

The use of wood (teak, bamboo and cane) lends an exotic touch to the inside finishings such as the ceilings, beams with hidden lights, curtains, counters, and other elements. For the main gates and bed headboards, wrought iron was most appropriate.

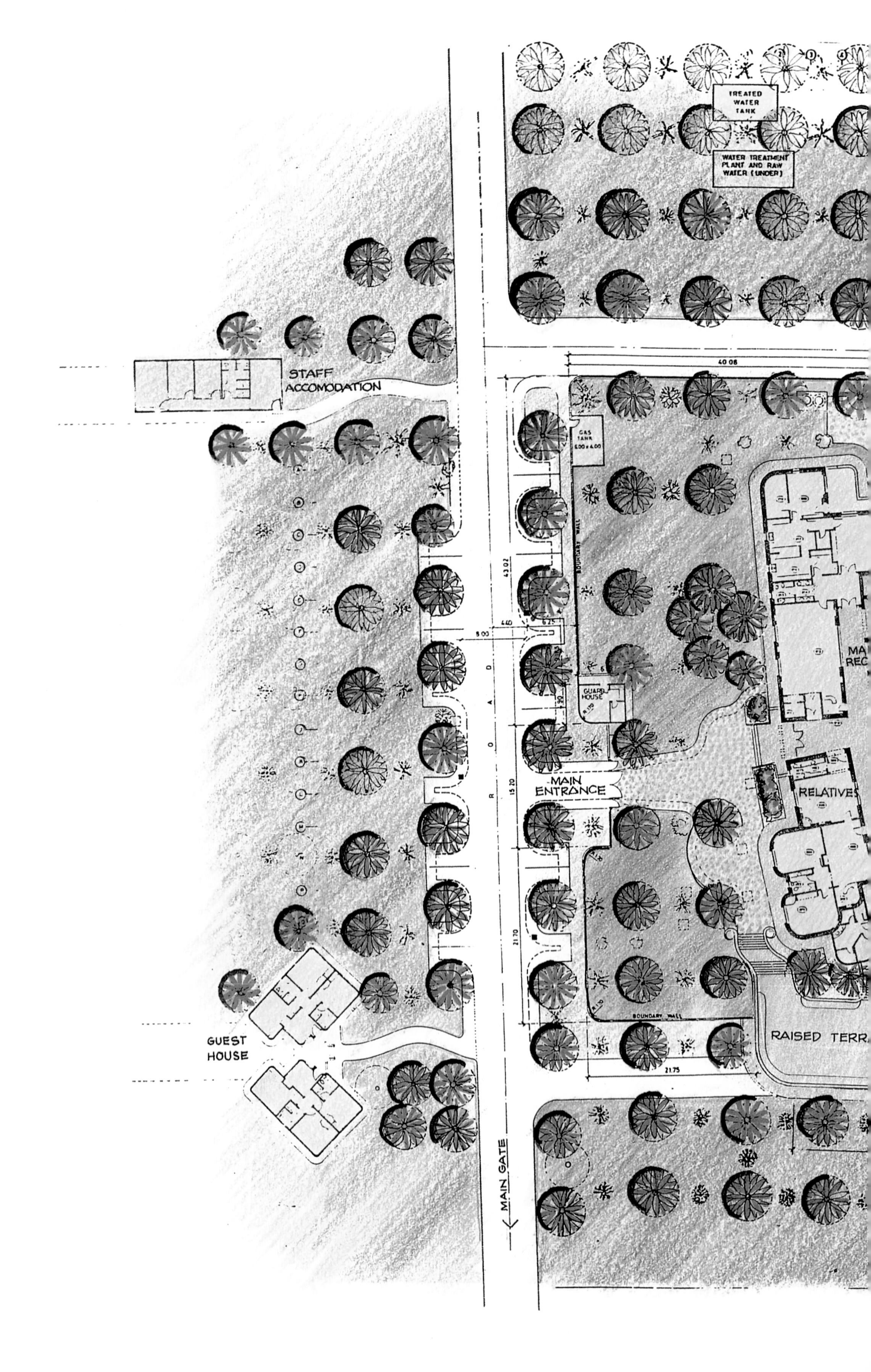
TREATED WATER TANK
WATER TREATMENT PLANT AND RAW WATER (UNDER)
STAFF ACCOMODATION
GAS TANK
GUARD HOUSE
MAIN ENTRANCE
ROAD
RELATIVES
BOUNDARY WALL
RAISED TERR
GUEST HOUSE
MAIN GATE

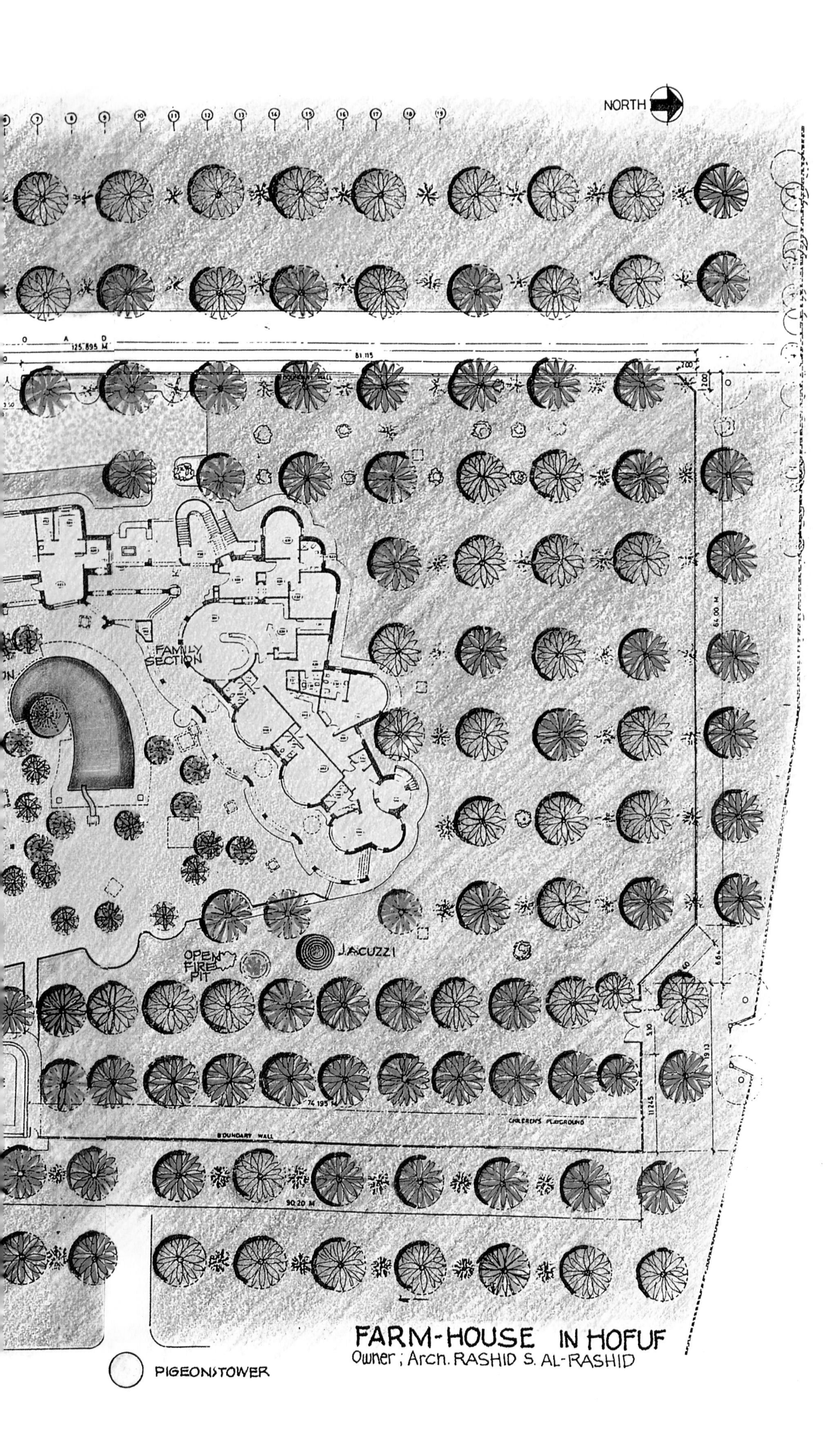
NORTH
FAMILY SECTION
OPEN FIRE PIT
JACUZZI
BOUNDARY WALL
CHILDREN'S PLAYGROUND
FARM-HOUSE IN HOFUF
Owner ; Arch. RASHID S. AL-RASHID
PIGEONSTOWER

FAHAD M. AL-SOLAIMAN

Riyadh, Saudi Arabia

A commercial and residential interior designer, Fahad Al-Solaiman graduated from King Saud University with a Bachelor of Architecture degree. Mr. Al-Solaiman's major projects include shops, showrooms and palaces throughout Saudi Arabia. He holds memberships in various clubs and professional societies. Mr. Al-Solaiman is presently a professional designer with the Saudi Arabia Standards Organization in Riyadh, Saudi Arabia.

"The primary design feature I wanted to to accomplish here in Dr. Alhamdan's villa was to overlap space to keep an open feel, yet define each space with its own separate identity and privacy. This was a particular challenge since the construction of the villa was originally done thirty years ago when development in Riyadh was in its earliest stages. Hence, renovation and interior design with an emphasis on creativity were the main target. With these goals in mind, I started studying the interior design of the whole villa and decided to combine simplicity with a modern style. Large glass windows and beautiful white aluminum screens around the exterior of the villa provide a wonderful transparency to the interior rooms. Red clay tile awnings provide sunshade for the glass. The curved natural stone steps to the entrance integrate with internal designs of the villa. Inside, granite tiles were used throughout in geometric patterns. Persian rugs were introduced to provide elegance in the reception room, where special attention was also given to the circular recess of the ceiling. Different elements of decorative gypsum ceiling were used throughout to give the impression of continuity.

To contact Fahad Al-Solaiman, telephone (966) 1-476-5893, or fax (966) 1-479-0581; Fahad's office is located at P.O. Box 26828, Riyadh 11496, Saudi Arabia.

PHOTOGRAPHY: MANSOON AHMED

LUCILLE ANDERSON

Munroe Falls, Ohio

A designer of commercial and residential interiors, Lucille Anderson graduated from the University of Akron in 1981. She founded Works of Wonder Interiors, where she is the owner and principal designer. Ms. Anderson's projects have been featured in numerous publications, such as *Builder/Architect, The Akron Beacon Journal, Small Business News* and *Best New Homes*. She is a philanthropist and an active member of several organizations including the Organization of Black Designers and the Builders Industry Association, and is an Interior Design Advisory Board Member at the University of Akron.

"After ten years of attending home shows, my clients finally brought to fruition the details for their 'dream home'. Her primary request was for yellow walls, accented with green – her favorite, energizing colors. The husband was partial to rose tones. Since they were starting with a blank canvas, these colors were infused into every room of their spacious traditional home, along with the unity of white carpet and painted woodwork. The ranch windows in the master bedroom presented a design dilemma which was solved by the expansive symmetrical window treatment shown here. Shades stack under the valance treatment to provide total blackout. Mahogany 18th century furnishings with brass drop bail hardware add to the richness of this wonderful, soft, yellow haven. The sitting area is graced by a beautiful rose-colored Chinese oriental rug. The master bath's white ceramic tile with green and rose inserts and its yellow floral wallcovering reinforce the melding of the personalities of this happy couple."

To contact Lucille Anderson, Allied ASID, call (330) 688-0969 or fax (330) 688-0155; Lucille's office is located at 265 North Main Street, Munroe Falls, Ohio 44262.

PHOTOGRAPHY: DON WEIMER

ANTHONY ANTINE

New York, New York

Noted interior designer Anthony Antine has worked in his field for over eighteen years. During this period, he has developed his signature style. Luxurious fabrics, rich colors and comfort are his primary focus. Trained as a couturier at the Fashion Institute of Technology, Mr. Antine created wardrobes for many of the most fashionable and discriminating people in the world, including such celebrities as Barbra Streisand. He now designs living environments for many of the same people. Works in progress include the restoration of a Mediterranean villa in Englewood, New Jersey; private residences for Robert Redford; an Adirondack style country house in the hills of Atami, Japan; a neo-classical house in downtown Tokyo; and a beach house in Malibu, California. A three-year refurbishing project of a two-hundred-foot yacht in Monaco and several residences in England, France, Korea, and Japan have spirited Antine to Europe and the Far East. This spring, he will be launching a line of furniture for Bexley Heath. Mr. Antine has also been recognized for his design work in various showhouses, including several in Southampton for the Rogers Memorial Library and the 1994 Kips Bay Showhouse. He continues the refurbishing of the Point Hotel in Saranac Lake, New York (the cover story for *Interior Design Magazine*). *Interior Design* and *Classic Home* featured his home in Palisade, New Jersey. Most recently, he has redone that home, and it is featured in the *Interior Design* October 1996 issue. Mr. Antine is a Founding Member of the ISID, New York Chapter.

"The photographs shown here are of my own private residence in New Jersey. I chose yellow and red as the theme for the living and dining rooms and liked it so much, I decided to carry it throughout the rest of the house. The accents of gold leaf add glamor, but, once again, comfort is the main concern in this project."

To contact Anthony Antine, call (212) 988-4096; Anthony's New York office is located at 200 East 77th, New York, New York 10021. His New Jersey office is located at 1028 Arcadian Way, Palisade, New Jersey 07024, phone (201) 224-0315 or fax (201) 224-5963.

PHOTOGRAPHY: PETER PAIGE

PERENNIALS
GUILD ON COLOR

SAMIR BADRO

Sharjah, United Arab Emirates

A native of Aleppo, Syria, Samir Badro took his Master's degree with honors in Architecture and Interior Design in 1970 from the Lebanese University School of Architecture and Interior Design. Fluent in Arabic, French and English, Mr. Badro spent the next several years working in Paris, Brussels and the United States. In 1975, Mr. Badro founded his own firm in Dubai U.A.E. where he has been established since.

Presently, he is chairman and chief executive officer of an international network of companies located in ten cities around the world, each being fully dedicated to interior design, as well as the manufacturing of custom furniture. Mr. Badro's project focus, though well known for palaces and elaborate residences for foreign dignitaries, has also comprised impressive corporate headquarters, major hotels, and luxury yachts.

"The challenging projects featured here are a luxury hotel suite in Edinburgh, Scotland, and an opulent residence on the river Thames, London. Both locations have similar cold climates, and yet I managed to evoke very different moods and ambiance in each. The hotel suite was created in earth tones and designed to shield guests from the outside freeze. Exotic woods keep their natural beauty in the glow of the warm palette, giving a subdued, traditional design. Below, the London residence is bright and spacious, and contrasts the gray darkness of the exterior. To achieve this look, accomplished painting techniques and elegant accents of gold leafing were used throughout."

To contact Samir Badro, call (971) 6-333-731 or fax (971) 6-332-650; Samir's office is located at P.O. Box 5835, Sharjah, United Arab Emirates.

VIORICA BELCIC

New York, New York

V-3 Design, an interior architectural firm, has offered a high level of experience and performance in New York, New Jersey and Connecticut for twenty-six years and specializes in commercial projects such as banks, law firms, and office spaces, as well as high-end residential interiors. The principal of the firm, Viorica Belcic, is a registered architect, A.I.A. member. She combines an extensive European background with a profound knowledge of classic art and design. Viorica enjoys working with demanding clients and looks upon meeting their requirements as an exciting challenge. The best of yesterday, today and tomorrow is synthesized in the melding of the art of architecture and decoration with practicality and beauty. Her work has been featured in numerous publications, including the *New York Times, Metropolitan Home, Unique Homes, Vogue International,* and *Showcase of Interior Design.*

"The formal living area below was created with ornamental moldings made of a new fibrous cast plaster and applied to the ceiling and walls. Lighting in front of the drapery emphasizes the richness of the fabric. On the opposite page, ribbon mahogany paneling was used in the residential library on the walls. The ceiling is papered in an antique gold finish while the antique alabaster chandelier and sconces give focus to the room. Finally, a free-standing circular mahogany staircase marks this townhouse entrance. We used local craftsmen for the exquisite ironwork balustrade. The large marble slab floor was a challenge in tailoring the pattern to the space and ensuring an exact fit."

To contact Viorica Belcic, call (212) 222-2551 or you may reach her by fax at (212) 222-2201; Viorica's office is located at 1212 Avenue of Americas, New York, New York 10036.

PHOTOGRAPHY: BILL ROTHCHILD

DOROTHY BOCCHINO, ASID

Saddle River, New Jersey

Dorothy Bocchino graduated from William Patterson College with a B.A. in Art, and later received a degree in Interior Design from the Interior Design Institute. Specializing in both residential and commercial design, Ms. Bocchino is a partner of both D'Image Associates, Inc. and Details & Design.

In addition to numerous private residences throughout the United States, she has designed the interiors of executive offices and model apartments throughout the East coast. Ms. Bocchino received the Design Award of Excellence in 1991, and is an Allied Member of the American Society of Interior Designers. Her projects have appeared in numerous publications including *Garden State Home and Garden, New Jersey Monthly, The New York Post*, and *The Record*.

"My clients are a happily married couple who work together in a family-owned skating rink. This is their master bedroom suite. Spending so much time together, and taking into consideration how hectic their lives are, this room was designed to be their haven. The warm color palette is soothing to the soul. The furniture reflects the classic yet masculine Empire style, comfortable to both husband and wife. Sumptuous silk draperies, which echo the vertically patterned wallcovering, soften the furniture's strong lines. The space includes a sitting room and sleeping area, as well as dressing room and home office."

To contact Dorothy Bocchino, call (201) 934-5420 or fax (201) 934-5597; Ms. Bocchino's office is located at 71 East Allendale Road, Saddle River, New Jersey 07458.

PHOTOGRAPHY: ROBERT FAULKNER

ANITA BROOKS INTERIOR DESIGN

Las Vegas, Nevada

The fresh, innovative look of Anita Brooks' design style has validated her reputation as a designer of first-class abilities and high standards of quality. Anita is known as a leading interior designer in Nevada and on the West Coast. Her work has been featured in professional magazines such as *The Designer, The Nevadan,* and *Designers West.* The American Society of Interior Designers awarded Anita the 1996 Design Excellence Award, as well as first place honors in several other categories, including her design of the luxury suites at the new Monte Carlo Hotel. She has also won first place Homer Awards in 1989, 1990, and 1991. Upon completion of her degree in Environmental Design from Brigham Young University, Ms. Brooks began her career in Orlando, Florida, with the notable design firm Southland Interiors. After returning to Las Vegas in 1973, she established Anita Brooks Interiors, Inc. Her current projects include exclusive residential homes, as well as work for the Luxor and Monte Carlo Hotels. Most notably, Anita and her design staff are working on the interior design of the Four Seasons Hotel and the Paradise Resort & Casino in Las Vegas.

"Old World style, reminiscent of palatial residences in the European manor, describe the family room below. Completely paneled in hand hewn and hand waxed pine, much of the detail is seen in the built-in entertainment center. Custom-designed area rugs, antiques, luxurious upholstery and one-of-a-kind accessories complete the room's ambience. The living room on the adjoining page has an Italian contemporary feel. The rich use of burnished velvet and distressed finishes on classic style furniture add to the flair. 17th and 18th century antiques create a palatial statement with a comfortable atmosphere."

To contact Anita Brooks Interiors, call (702) 364-5888 or fax (702) 364-0503; Anita's office is located at 4270 S. Cameron Avenue, Suite 1, Las Vegas, Nevada 89103.

PHOTOGRAPHY: MARY E. NICHOLS (*left*), JEFFREY GREEN (*above*)

GIACOMETTI

MICHAEL DE SANTIS, ASID

New York, New York

Michael de Santis is an internationally renowned residential and commercial interior designer. Because of his worldwide recognition, he has participated in numerous design showcase homes. His interiors have graced the covers of *Architectural Digest* and *Interior Design*, and his work has appeared in all the leading American interior design publications. Past first prize winner of the famous Hexter Award, Mr. de Santis has also received the Award for Excellence in Residential Design at the Chicago Design Fest.

"The residence shown below and opposite is a contemporary interpretation of Anglo-Indian design style, comprising a neutral palette with teak and cane accents. The light and airy brightness is achieved through sheer gauze curtains and stuccoed linen walls. The honed Arcadia marble floors are accented with glazed terra cotta tiles. The sitting room in the master bedroom of the Rogers Memorial Library Showhouse in Southampton featured on the next page is relaxed, understated, yet invitingly sophisticated. Ivory and white panels are accented by the *faux bois* paint application along the underside of the crown moulding and on the mantel panel. White pique slipcovered seating is offset with formal marquetry furniture. Linen shades trimmed with tassel fringe lend a breezy softness, while the 19th century Aubusson rug brings inside the lush greenery beyond. The final room is a Ritz Tower Hotel residence in New York. Traditional elements and contemporary accents are combined in this apartment. The muted lighting and the warm, soft colors enhance the clients' art collection, as well as complement the decor's Oriental undertones. Plush seating in chenilles and silk satins add glamour. The library and living room come together through the use of pocketed doors to allow for entertaining."

To contact Michael de Santis, call (212) 753-8871 or fax (212) 935-7777; Michael's office is located at 1110 Second Avenue at 58th Street, New York, New York 10022.

Kennedys
IACOCCA
MEN OF MEN
TOM WOLFE

DECORATION USA
INTERIOR DESIGN AND DECORATION
INTERIOR DECORATION
THE Straw Man
The Wilderling
CLAIRE LORRIMER
Family Trade
James Carroll
CENTURY
PORTRAITS
THE WITCHES OF EASTWICK
FOURTH MAN
EN ICE

SUELLEN DEFRANCIS

New York, New York

Suellen DeFrancis, Design Principal of her own firm, has offices in Manhattan, Tokyo and Scarsdale, New York, where she resides. Prior to establishing her own office, she spent two years at John Burgee Architects with Philip Johnson. She has broken new ground in Japan practicing there as a Western woman architect and as a member of the Far East Society of Architects and Engineers.

Ms. DeFrancis holds a Masters degree in Urban Design, a Bachelors degree in Architecture and a Bachelor of Science in Architecture. She received the del Gaudio Award for Total Design Excellence from the New York Society of Architects and a New York Chapter AIA scholarship for Graduate Study. Suellen DeFrancis recently renovated the gothic-style castle at Tarrytown, recreating baronial guest rooms and extraordinary restaurants, providing custom furniture and finishes to suit the historic atmosphere.

"The interiors of the castle enhance the original architecture and complement its history. The castle's majestic stone carved fireplaces, 17th century French paneling and lush tapestries carry visitors back through time. We restored and reused the original Renaissance Revival-style furniture, such as carved oak side chairs, used as desk chairs and occasional chairs. The built-in sideboard with carved columns and canopy, built-in china cabinet, and fireplace mantle carved in the shape of a boar's head are now striking features of the Oak Room Restaurant. New upholstered chairs are graced by a reproduced medieval tapestry. The eclectic art collection includes 19th century prints and paintings, gothic carved panels, medieval marble sculptures and original silk woven European wall tapestries dating back to 1600. A combination of Durkan patterned carpets and Oriental rugs warm the stone entryway. Custom lighting fixtures designed to fit the period impart a soft glow. Guest suites have ornate fireplaces imported from England. Gothic windows overlook the Hudson River. The suites are individually decorated with antiques and gothic-style furnishings. Even in the splendor of a gothic castle, we designed the rooms for people to feel comfortable and enjoy their surroundings."

To contact Suellen DeFrancis, call (212) 879-8386; her main office is located at 900 Park Avenue, New York, New York, with additional offices in Scarsdale, New York, and Tokyo, Japan.

DIWAN INTERIORS

Salmiah, Kuwait

Diwan Interiors International is an interior design and contracting firm which was founded in 1987. Despite the turmoil that Kuwait experienced in 1990, Diwan Interiors has been involved in many unique and exclusive projects, and has successfully completed an array of prestigious projects for their clients. Egyptian architect Iman Harby, Managing Partner, has been working as a professional interior designer for the past fifteen years. Ms. Harby received her Bachelor of Architecture degree from the Faculty of Engineering at Cairo University in Egypt in 1980. Fouad Nassar, another principal of the company, graduated from Cairo University with a Bachelor's degree in Architecture in 1975. Mr. Nassar's design experience spans numerous countries where his design concepts range from extremely conservative and classical to contemporary and completely innovative.

"This concrete building was taken over by the Iraqi military, turning it into ruins. Upon retreat of the troops, the client asked for a re-design of the interior and landscaping. With the addition of a two-story atrium space at the main entrance followed by a series of defined areas, it symbolizes the openness of the floor plan while maintaining the privacy and function of each space. Unpolished Australian stone flooring is used to complement the matte finished cherrywood doors and woodwork. Indeed, this house has come out after the 'storm' with a totally new, fresh spirit."

To contact Diwan Interiors, call (965) 574-8765 or fax (965) 574-8760; the office is located in Ras Salmiah, Salem Al-Mubarak St., 1/F, Wataniah Complex. The mailing address is P.O. Box 2071, Salmiah 22021, Kuwait.

PHOTOGRAPHY: UWE WRUCK

LOVEJOY DURYEA, ASID, IIDA, IDEC

New York, New York

Lovejoy Duryea is a master of interpreting European and American style to create sumptuous interiors, producing homes of great elegance, comfortable family spaces, or fresh, simple smart ones. Her formal interior design studies include honors work at Parsons School of Design and Master's work at Pratt Institute in New York. In 1980, she founded Dorset Design, Inc., which has become known for helping clients achieve a confident and personal style. Her company undertakes commissions worldwide. Projects range from opulent Park Avenue apartments, to transforming a stone farmhouse in the south of France.

"Mrs. Duryea has an extensive knowledge of art, antiques, fabrics, finishes. In the last two years, Lovejoy Duryea's ideas and work have been featured in over 200 newspapers and magazines, including the *New York Times*, the *Greenwich Times, Professional Designer, Interiors and Sources*, as well as several network and cable TV broadcasts. She is a Professional Member and past New York Board Member of IIDA and of ASID, and is both NCIDQ certified and certified by the State of New York. She is a Founder and Chair of the Interior Design Department at the School of Visual Arts in New York City.

"The project in these photos was a complete renovation of a Park Avenue duplex. In a tight, confined space, a new staircase and railing was created, utilizing principles based on the golden section. A maid's room was removed to create a new, larger and more gracious dining room. Mirrored French doors reflect the view of Central Park. On the opposite page, the carefully selected moldings and trim, plus the addition of columns between the foyer and the living room, creates a vista that frames and culminates on the *chinoiserie* secretary breakfront in the living room. The pale pink marble of the foyer reiterates the black and pink theme of the wrought iron staircase railing. The project team consisted of Interior Design and Team Leader: Lovejoy Duryea; Project Architect: David Nahon; Contractor: I. Mass and Sons; Lighting: Bob Friedman of Lampyridae."

Lovejoy Duryea may be reached at either Dorset Design Inc., 372 Fifth Avenue, Suite 8F, New York, New York 10018, phone (212) 290-2299, fax (212) 714-1943; or the Interior Design Department School of Visual Arts, 209 East 23rd St., New York, New York 10010, phone (212) 592-2572 or fax (212) 592-2573, e-mail: lduryea@adm.schoolofvisualarts.edu.

PHOTOGRAPHY: SCOTT DORRANCE

ANTIQUE FURNITURE
WINSLOW HOMER
John James Audubon

TRELLIS
JAMIE GARNOCK
TRELLIS
Newport Houses
Photographs by Roberto Schezen

WILLIAM R. EUBANKS

Memphis, Tennessee

Memphis, Tennessee and New York City are the home bases of interior designer William Eubanks. Upon completion of his degree in interior design, Mr. Eubanks established his own firm in 1976. His Georgian style showroom is enhanced by fine 17th, 18th, and early 19th century English and Continental antiques which, for him, are natural tools of the trade.

"Ivory glazed moldings with soft brown walls of the living room featured on the opposite page create a background for the dramatically colored damask of salmon, ivory and gold cotton. The Louis XV mirror adds another dimension while Flemish cushions add texture. This combination creates a warm Continental ambience. Below, the warm tortoiseshell finished moldings and ochre walls enhance the dining room filled with George III and Regency antiques. The following page features a Louis XVI-style Chinese red library designed for clients who love color. The brilliant colors were all transferred from the oushak carpet. The yellow golds add warmth and friendliness. Overall, a blending of periods and styles are juxtaposed to create a timeless yet friendly space."

To contact William Eubanks, call (901) 272-1825 or fax (901) 272-1845; Mr. Eubank's office is located at 1516 Union Avenue, Memphis, Tennessee 38104. In New York, call (212) 753-1842.

PHOTOGRAPHY: LANGDON CLAY

NAGLAA ASAAD FARSI

Jeddah, Saudi Arabia

Naglaa Asaad Farsi completed her studies in interior design and silver and gold embroidery in 1990. During the course of her studies, she completed a detailed research of the traditional techniques of practically all the cultural forms of expression and art. Ms. Farsi then started her own design and embroidery on canvas, silk, cotton, wood, satin and many other materials. The interior design section of her business specializes in residential projects as well as the creation of custom stained glass. Mrs. Farsi has recently opened a branch in Europe located in Sion, Wallis, Switzerland.

"This grand salon was designed in traditional Islamic style with regard to architecture and the room's decor. An ornate mantel framing the fireplace has a marble top which holds prized, rare silver vases and other favorite mementos. The detailed edges of the screen perfectly complement the shape and elegance of the fireplace. The ceiling enhances the scope and dimension of the space while Oriental rugs, together with three sofas arranged in a conversational setting, complete the overall design. Opulent columns and capstones integrate design elements providing a beautiful backdrop for the round Napoleon table and elegantly encasing the mirrored wall, completing the relaxed and luxurious feel of the entire room."

To reach Naglaa Farsi in Europe, you may contact her at Silver Branch, Post Office Box 772, Immeuble Le Grillon, Rue des Creusets 32, 1950 Sion, Switzerland; telephone (41) 27-323-42-25, fax (41) 27-323-42-26. To reach Mrs. Farsi in Saudi Arabia, contact her at Silver Branch, Post Office Box 2525, 21461 Jeddah, Saudi Arabia; telephone (966) 2-654-64-64, fax (966) 2-654-99-45.

LAURA GOOMAS, ALLIED ASID

Saddle River, New Jersey

Laura Goomas was educated at the Interior Design Institute in New Jersey. An Allied Member of the American Society of Interior Designers, she is currently a partner in both D'Image Associates, Inc. and Details and Design, a gift and accessory shop in Saddle River. Ms. Goomas' work has appeared in many publications, including *Showcase of Interior Design, Garden State Home & Garden, Dream Kitchens, Good Housekeeping Magazine, Family Circle, Contemporary Stone Design, Design New Jersey* and *The Bergen Record.* She is also the author of articles appearing in both *New Jersey Goodlife* and *Design New Jersey*.

In 1991, Ms. Goomas received the Design Award for Excellence from *Garden State Home & Garden* for a master bedroom suite. Her work has been featured in many of the New York/New Jersey area's most prestigious showhouses. A space designed with her partners for the 1994 Mansions in May received the "Best Room in Show" award. Most recently, the partners created a kitchen with Old World charm that was a highlight of the 1996 Oak & Ivy Showhouse.

"Although we all admire grand spaces, living in them can be disconcerting. Vaulted ceilings create the impression of unconfined space, an illusion which makes many people uncomfortable. This is particularly true for private spaces such as bedrooms and family rooms. In this family room, a soffit and companion *trompe l'oeil* balustrade provide the visual anchor that keeps the ceiling from floating away. Warm earth tones gently envelop all who enter. A table lamp and coffee table, two treasured possessions that once graced the home of the client's mother, were lovingly refurbished with silver leaf. In this new setting, they bestow an abiding sense of family history and serve as inspiration for the silver touches elsewhere in the room. Deceptively durable fabrics, including chenille sofa and animal skin tapestry wing chairs, make this room exceedingly livable.

"This cozy, comfortable kitchen has ample room for an active family and plenty of space for serious cooking. The soft country decor and knotty pine cabinetry are the perfect complements to the home's gracious colonial architecture. The gentle rose, khaki and cream color scheme creates the illusion that the sun's warm rays are always streaming in through the softly dressed windows. Corian countertops service the perimeter, while granite tops the island. Handcrafted tiles surrounded by tumbled marble form the backsplash that overlooks a six burner Dacor cooktop. Practical touches include the double sink, double Thermador ovens and sweep-clean Mexican tile floor. Handpainted vines, inspired by the fabric at the windows, enhance the domed ceiling in the breakfast area, while a *faux* fence, complete with pineapple posts to symbolize hospitality, defines the back staircase."

To contact Laura Goomas, call (201) 934-5420 or fax (201) 934-5597; Laura's office is located at 71 East Allendale Road, Saddle River, New Jersey 07458.

PHOTOGRAPHY: ROBERT I. FAULKNER

AMR. AHMED HAFEZ

Alexandria, Egypt

Architect and interior designer Amr. Ahmed Hafez graduated from the Faculty of Engineering in Alexandria in 1984. He has worked in architectural and interior design offices in Alexandria and Basel, Switzerland. Mr. Hafez opened his own design firm in 1986, specializing in residential and corporate offices, shops and exhibitions throughout Egypt. His primary objective is to reflect the aspirations and personalities of each client's individuality and to give each project a completely different and special identity of its own.

"The vice president's room featured below reflects an elegant combination of the traditional, the archeological and the avante garde. The juxtaposition of extraordinary finishing, antique materials and ultra-modern glazing in the facade harmonizes to produce a mysterious, thought-provoking quality. To deepen the room's mystery, the post-modern lamp and French classic painting were added. Richness is achieved by using Egyptian green marble in between the oak floor, while the application of French stone on the walls implies a modern interpretation of classical style.

"The second project shown in the photo to the right is the entranceway of a major contractor's firm. The challenge was to transform this classic apartment into one of the most modern and impressive offices in Alexandria. Informal elegance defines this gracious and inviting environment. Using architectural features such as marble columns, beautifully marbleized cornice, glass block walls, and magnificent oak doors enhances the warm ele-gance and refinement of this entrance. Stepping through the doorway, the viewer's focus is drawn to the grandeur of the iron door, leading into the meeting room. A series of lines continue to enhance the hall's height. Choosing a warm palette kept the hall bright and cheerful. As a final touch, the logo of the group is engraved in the back wall behind the reception counter, creating an elegant balance with the ceiling above."

To contact Amr. Ahmed Hafez, call (20) 3-848-884, or fax his office at (20) 3-586-8710; Ahmed's office is located at 5 El Kes Abadeer, Roushdy, Alexandria, Egypt.

LOTUS
LOTUS
GROUP OF
COMPANIES

CONSTANCE W. HUMMEL, IIDA

Barrington, Illinois

Constance Hummel is the current President of the International Interior Design Association, Illinois Chapter. She has been an Interior Designer for twenty years and holds a B.A. degree from Florida State University and an M.A. from Northwestern University. Constance has studied at the Harrington Institute of Interior Design and briefly at the Inchbald School in London. She is licensed and practices both residential and commercial design. An Honorary Doctorate was bestowed upon Constance in June by the International Academy.

Her projects are quite varied, and include the lobby of American Can Company in Barrington, Illinois, a travel agency in the Chicago suburbs, many insurance offices, Century 21 Realty office design in Arlington Heights, Illinois, and residences in Lake Point Tower, Chicago, Illinois, and various sites throughout the country. She owns her own design firm, Winston Scott Interiors, which is located in Barrington, Illinois. Constance has had projects published in the *Chicago Tribune*, the *Chicago Sun-Times, Pioneer Press*, and her work is featured in Vincé Floors brochures, as well as *Chicago Home Book* and many other publications. Her design philosophy is: appropriateness, function, and beauty must blend in order for excellence in design to emerge.

"The private residence featured here is located on the Gold Coast of Chicago. This couple requested a contemporary environment in keeping with the architecture of the building, but they wanted it to be softened with a few eclectic accent pieces. The wife wanted durable and easily cleanable surfaces, and both husband and wife preferred a color palette of gray, black and white. Our firm had designed this couple's suburban residence fifteen years ago."

To contact Constance Hummel, please call (847) 304-1010 or fax (847) 304-1040. Her office is located in Barrington, Illiniois, and consultations are by appointment only.

PHOTOGRAPHY: HEDRICH-BLESSING

TWENTIETH-CENTURY MODERN MASTERS
QUARRY
LINCOLN KIRSTEIN

FREDERIC JOCHEM

New York, New York

Since 1989, Frederic Jochem Architectural Interiors has provided clients with a high level of personal service and award winning design solutions to a wide variety of projects in the United States and abroad. With experience in planning, architecture, landscape and interior design, Frederic Jochem lends his sense of expertise in program development and project administration for major projects, including his current project decorating a house in Casa del Campo on the island of the Dominican Republic. Mr. Jochem's European approach to decorating is one of total collaboration with the client. He works to create a pleasurable environment which reflects the client's own taste and personality. With an intrinsic sense of serenity, Frederic's philosophy invites the mind to be open and versatile, expressing a unique and eclectic style of decorating. Together, the designer and client achieve a dynamic mix of tradition with a twist.

"This selection of photographs depicts the drawing room of a Beekman Place apartment in New York, a sitting room in a Left Bank townhouse in Paris, and a living room in a historical house in Bermuda. While the New York apartment underwent extensive renovations, the challenge was integrating one of America's most important art collections from the Rockefeller family into an art deco apartment in today's lifestyle. The main focus for the Paris townhouse was to respect the periods of the furnishings and upholstery, keeping them in harmony with the architecture. As for Hinson Hall, a Bermudian historical house, the important aspect of the project was to adapt the taste of the client to the appropriate environment and climate."

To contact Frederic Jochem, call (212) 956-1840 or fax (212) 956-1845; Frederic's office is located at 240 Central Park South, New York, New York, 10019.

PHOTOGRAPHY: JENNIFER LEVEY/JOHN HALL

Picasso
WATTEAU

PETER JÖHNK

Hamburg, Germany

Peter Jöhnk, Innenarchitekt, established his firm in 1984. His team of highly skilled professionals excel at integrating a full range of interior design services, project management, and corporate identity consulting. Their specific strength lies in the creativity and understanding they bring to various hotel projects, with a scope of expertise which encompasses lobby design; restaurant, bar, café, lounge and food court concepts; fitness and wellness centers; as well as guest room and bathroom planning.

Mr. Jöhnk's primary goal is to create a special feeling for every project in order to make it unique. There is no specific Peter Jöhnk style – instead, each project is endowed with its own character and sense of time, place, and function. Regardless of the size of a project, an overriding theme is thoughtfully researched and developed which will capture the true emotions of present and future alike.

"Special projects featured here were all completed in Germany and include the foyer and restaurant of the Holiday Inn Crowne Plaza, Hotel St. Raphael, the Celler Hof foyer, a Spreebogen shopping mall, a Villa M bathroom, Bagel Restaurant, Young Budget Bank, and the exquisite detail of a banister in Spreebogen, Berlin."

To contact Peter Jöhnk, call (49) 40-68-94-21-0 or fax (49) 40-68-94-21-30; Peter's office is located at Wandsbeker, Königstrasse 50, 22041 Hamburg, Germany.

PHOTOGRAPHY: CHRISTIAN KERBER

MODE & ACCESSOIRE
BOOS
MODELADEN
LINE
frohe festtage
VISA
EUROCARD

REZEPTION

CHIP JOHNSTON, ASID, IFDA

Atlanta, Georgia

Residential projects are the focus of Chip Johnston's Atlanta-based interior design firm. Educated at Emory University and the University of North Carolina at Chapel Hill, Mr. Johnston gained valuable interior design experience before opening his own firm in 1979. As a Professional Member of the American Society of Interior Designers, he has received a number of accolades from his peers, including an Industry Foundation Citation, a Medalist Award and three Presidential Citations. His memberships in the National Trust for Historic Preservation and several fine arts organizations speak highly of his commitment to a cultured approach to every project.

"Our favorite artist added some trees inside, echoing the profusion of plants outdoors, in this marble-floored solarium overlooking a pool below and an adjacent deck. The late John Carsman's 'Giverny' series prints are featured, adding color to the striped loveseat and floral cushions of the rattan chairs. The next room featured is the foyer to a master suite. A custom-striped wallcovering complements the antique bench, Oriental rug, and chandelier, while a portion of a collection of watercolors grace the walls. On the next page are two views of the business home of an internationally active CEO who enjoys the panorama of the extensively forested office building setting. Finally, the scrolled shell of a lavatory pedestal in a powder room adds relief from the plain wainscoting. The three-light sconce gives a soft glow to the intricate design of the upper wallcovering."

To contact Chip Johnston, call (404) 231-4141 or fax (404) 261-3713; Chip's office is located at 2996 Grandview Avenue N.E., Suite 300, Atlanta Georgia 30305-3245.

PHOTOGRAPHY: DAVID SCHILLING

Irish houses & castles

JUDITH SISLER JOHNSTON, ASID

Jacksonville, Florida

After receiving her Bachelor of Arts degree from Keane College in New Jersey, Judith Sisler Johnston obtained her Master of Arts degree from Truman State University in Missouri. Currently, Ms. Johnston serves as president of Sisler-Williams Interior Design in Jacksonville, Florida, which opened in 1985. She is an Allied Member of the American Society of Interior Designers. Her work has received national recognition, with numerous awards in residential, country club and model home competitions.

"The showhomes depicted on the following pages were specifically designed to appeal to a resort home clientele and to reflect the diverse tastes and interests which are found in a professionally decorated custom home. I chose a neutral backdrop for the tropical design shown here and layered it with different textures of limestone, tumbled marble, natural fibers and textiles. Then I decided to contrast the monochromatic palette with colorful tapestries and prints, vivid tile patterns and strong accent paints to achieve a delicate balance between elegant and casual. The use of custom millwork and interior architecture reinforce the emphasis on detail from floor to ceiling.

"In the neo-classic model, I blended iron, glass, and painted and lacquered wood elements to reflect a timeless sense of classic European design. The hand-carved furniture is richly upholstered in contrasting silks and tapestries. The lavish window treatments were designed to frame and complement the tropical landscape surround."

To contact Judith Sisler Johnston, call (904) 363-0177, or fax (904) 363-9980; Judith's office is located at 9143 Phillips Highway, Suite 260, Jacksonville, Florida 32256.

PHOTOGRAPHY: LAWRENCE TAYLOR

Toulouse-Lautrec

PAYAL KAPOOR

New Delhi, India

Payal Kapoor joined the New Delhi Polytechnic Interiors School in 1987 and, after graduation, was handpicked by the Executive Director of Mansara, one of the leading interior design houses in the country whose specialty involves major five-star hotels including the Oberoi Hotels. Ms. Kapoor's talent then led her to a challenging position as Senior Advisor of Dream City. Under Payal's direct supervision, the company diversified from making doors and windows to manufacturing excellent quality furniture. As a result, Dream City was then able to successfully execute a wide number of projects on a turnkey basis.

Wanting to expand her creativity and identity as an interior designer, Payal Kapoor launched her own design firm, Visions, in 1991. The company's area of expertise encompasses hotels, resorts, institutes, schools, corporate offices, residences and farmhouses. She maintains a complete staff of designers and a factory which manufactures their own furniture.

In the concept of interiors, the harmonic blend of materials and colors, coupled with the visual effects of various themes, is key to the company's designs. Visions makes no compromises, and concepts are discussed, explained, researched, and rediscussed in order to please their clients. Ms. Kapoor's projects in India and abroad have appeared in numerous publications. Notable works include the G.D. Goenka Public School and Umaid Bhawan Palace Hotel in Jodhpur. She is also a contributing writer for the decor section of a leading New Delhi newspaper. With her design team, Payal completed the interior design of the mobile luxury hotel featured here.

"The Palace on Wheels is a new broad gauge train which was commissioned by the Government of India and the Tourism Department of Rajasthan to be run as a five-star luxury mobile hotel for rich tourists desiring to cover the 'Gateway of India'. The old train, owned by the Maharajas, has been taken off the tracks of Indian railways. Fourteen passenger coaches – each with the distinctive decor of a former princely state of Rajasthan – two dining coaches, and a lounge car were completely transformed. In the bedroom of the Kota State Room, two single beds display inlay work in three types of wood. The intricately carved *jharokha* is reflected through the mirror on the opposing wall, while the ceiling frescoes are painted in vibrant greens as found in the palaces of Rajasthan. The bar and lounge is also used as a dance area, conference hall, and reading room. Behind the counter is a large panel of stained glass depicting two peacocks. The color scheme, revolving around the blues and greens of the peacock, is especially evident overhead. The ceiling boasts the exquisite work of over one hundred painted glass pieces and highlights the muted sandy colors of the upholstery. For the Bikaner State Lounge, the color scheme was inspired by opulent coronation rooms and done in glowing reds and golds. A royal crest is highlighted in gold embroidery work on the valance. Relief work and a canvas oil painting provide the backdrop for the ceiling."

To contact Payal Kapoor, call (91) 11-610-7522, 11-619-6115 fax (91) 11-619-3570 or e-mail ajay.vintage@axcess.net.in and ajayk@giasdl01.vsnl.net.in; Payal's office is located at A-1/140, Safdarjung Enclave, New Delhi, India 110029.

PHOTOGRAPHY: NITIN UPADHYE

india

NANCY KWOK, MCSD

Hong Kong, China

Nancy Kwok was educated at Hong Kong Polytechnic and is a member of the Chartered Society of Designers. Ms. Kwok formed her practice, Hinex Universal Design Consultants Company Limited, in 1986 and has successfully completed many remarkable and sizable design projects, including the Macau Headquarters Building of the Xinhua News Agency, the Shenzhen Headquarters Building of the Bank of China, the Gloria Plaza Hotels in Beijing, Shenyang and Dailian, the seven story Oriental Rainbow Department Store in Shenzhen, the Top Glory Headquarters Building in Hong Kong, and numerous branches of Citibank and Dah Sing Bank throughout Hong Kong.

"My design intent and approach for this project, the Standard Chartered Bank, was to create an environment that was efficient, comfortable, and inviting. The floor space is divided into four sections, with each section visually connected and conveniently accessible by every customer while still retaining a sense of privacy between the activities in neighboring zones. The Welcome Section pictured below is prominently located next to the main entrance and the main staircase, serving as the first contact point with the customers. The Consultation Section, shown in the photo on the adjoining page, demonstrates how the space was efficiently utilized to meet the bank's requirement that customers feel a sense of privacy when conducting their personal financial transactions. This is accomplished with the use of color changes in the flooring, ceiling drop soffits which visually separate the space from other sections of the bank, orientation of the furniture, and the integrated conference table work areas.

"Visual interest was dramatically heightened in the photos on the following pages by the use of offset display angles on the Merchandising Wall which invite the customer to move along the wall, gleaning information at each station. The design allows the bank's staff a comfortable view of the customer so that they can assist and give advice to viewers when appropriate. The stairway is a combination of efficient, elegant, and classic design elements which draw the client to avail themselves of the bank's personal finance services upstairs. The timeless juxtaposition of natural wood handrails, heavy wrought iron detailing, and white marble flooring convey a contemporary, yet substantial feel to the bank's special customers."

To contact Nancy Kwok, call (852) 2-589-0700 or contact her by fax at (852) 2-589-0708; Nancy's office is located at Room 1302, Wealthy Industrial Building, 22-26 Wing Yip Street, Kwai Chung, Hong Kong.

高貸款額
低息優惠
Personal Financial Services

MERCURY
SELECTED
TRUST
MERCURY
investment services

LA MAISON FLEURIE, INC.

Palm Beach, Florida

Annick Presles apprenticed with Countess Jacqueline de Ribes in Spain and France before opening La Maison Fleurie, Inc. in Caracas in 1985. Four years later, she and partner Sophie-Eve Hocquard opened their second studio in Palm Beach, Florida. Specializing in residential, commercial and party design, their many projects include the decoration of the American Society Ball in honor of David Rockefeller, the celebration for Venezuelan President Carlos Andres Perez, and the American Red Cross Showcase in Palm Beach in 1990, 1991, 1994, 1996 and 1997; also, the Norton Museum of Art Showcase for the Art of Beautiful Table Settings in 1995, 1996, and 1997. They have established a fine clientele all over the world.

"The former structure of this house had high windows and open walls; so to create a livable space with human proportions, we added walls and reduced the height of the windows with wood and bamboo shades. Each room carefully complements the other with a palette of colors and materials such as wood, metal and glass.

"The entrance had a large white door that now is painted in *faux bois*. For the bar, the wall was widened and squares of shimmering glass were applied to give a gentle effect. The frame is made of wood and large metal nails to accentuate my client's crystal collection. Brazilian furniture and a painted floor adorn the alfresco room. In the dining room, an oversize chandelier was chosen to balance the height of the ceiling. Ambient browns harmonize with the blinds in the guest bedroom to create a warm, intimate atmosphere."

To contact Annick Presles, call (561) 833-1083 or fax (561) 833-9318; Annick's office is located at The Paramount, 139 North County Road, Suite 25, Palm Beach, Florida 33480.

PHOTOGRAPHY: BRANTLEY PHOTOGRAPHY

DONALD W. LILLY, ASID

Jupiter, Florida

Donald Lilly, ASID, has become one of the most highly sought after interior designers in the country with major projects in the United States, the Caribbean, Europe and Saudi Arabia. He has been recognized and published in national trade and consumer magazines and international hard-cover books. Since founding his firm in Jupiter, Florida, in 1988, he has since opened offices in Miami and at the ultra-exclusive Ocean Reef Club in Key Largo, Florida, where he and his family have been members for twenty-five years. This young multi-award winning design firm specializes in luxury residential, model show homes, commercial, nautical and resort projects. Mr. Lilly was educated in Fine Art at Western Maryland College prior to graduating cum laude from the Art Institute of Ft. Lauderdale with a degree in Interior Design. He is a licensed interior designer, a Professional Member of the American Society of Interior Designers, and has been featured in *Who's Who in Interior Design* since 1988. His diversified clientele includes Fortune 500 executives, celebrities and professional sports figures.

"To create the dramatic effects achieved in both of these luxurious residences, a unique combination of interior architectural detailing, dramatic lighting, and age-old finishing techniques on furnishings and wall surfaces was applied. On the facing page, saturnia stone floors are inlayed with Italian marble. Sweeping hand-forged iron staircases lead to the private guest suites. The pecky cypress vaulted beam ceiling, antique chandelier and rich textured fabrics of silk chenille and tapestry add authenticity and elegance to this Italian Renaissance living area. The following pages depict the one-of-a-kind finishes and features that are further enhanced with the addition of dramatic lighting. In the dining area, a custom inlayed, imported Italian mosaic is reflected in the lighted coffered ceiling detail which boasts a *trompe l'oeil* illusion of sky and balustrade. In the living room, recessed wall niches, exotic finishes and decorative iron appliqués create a dramatic backdrop for the sophisticated and inviting fabrics. In the master bath, large stone columns frame the entry as his and hers frameless glass enclosed showers flank the enormous Roman tub. In another master suite, the fanciful *trompe l'oeil* mural behind the hand forged iron headboard is flanked by custom iron sconces. In the family/media room, subtle faux finished walls and ceiling complement the dramatic architectural details that adorn this elegant room. State-of-the-art audio/video components are hidden behind the large retractable doors. I feel what sets us apart from other design firms is our ability to take the project from preliminary planning stages through the final installation. Careful planning with the client, builder, and architect from the project's inception enables us to create unique interior architectural details, dramatic/functional lighting, and provisions for state-of-the-art, fully automated spaces. Ultimately, we are creating highly customized surroundings for exquisite furnishings, fabrics, and artwork."

To contact Donald Lilly, call (561) 746-5010 or fax (561) 743-4398; Donald's office is located at River Plaza, 900 S. U.S. Highway One, Suite 303, Jupiter, Florida 33477. In Miami, call (305) 253-0550 or fax (305) 253-2552, located at 7241 S.W. 168th Street, Suite C, Miami, Florida 33157. To contact his Ocean Reef Club office, call (305) 367-4888 or fax (305) 367-2817, located at 100 Anchor Drive #400, Key Largo, Florida 33037. Project Assistants: Julie Yamuk, ASID Allied; Kathryn Timmerman, ASID Allied. Project Builders: Provident Construction Co.; Simmons Building Corporation. Project Architects: Kunick & Associates; Armin Wessel/Peacock & Lewis.

PHOTOGRAPHY: JERRY MACFARLAND

THE GREAT MASTERS
RENOIR

RICARDO MAYER, ASID, AIA

Rio de Janeiro, Brazil

Born in Rio de Janeiro, Ricardo Mayer applies his knowledge of architecture and interior design to each of his commercial, retail and residential projects. Mr. Mayer studied at the Instituto La Fayette and National University before establishing his architectural firm in 1970. He is a Professional Member of the American Society of Interior Designers, as well as a member of the Cooper-Hewitt Museum in New York, the National Trust for Historic Preservation, and the Construction Specifications Institute (CSI). Mr. Mayer holds a Ph.D. in Interior Design from Southern California University (SCUPS), and his architectural and interior designs have been featured in numerous publications, including *Casa e Decoracao, Casa e Jardin, Casa Claudia, Arquitetura e Construcao* and *Casa Vogue*.

"Situated outside Rio de Janeiro in the mountainous region of Teresopolis, this sixteen hundred square meter residence was designed to be in complete harmony with the surrounding landscape. While some elements of the architectural design are reminiscent of a Georgian style, the home offers its own particular elegance with a combination of stonework, brickwork, wood, and metal. The main entrance is positioned under the primary terrace which adjoins the living room and, thereby, provides a central access to the living area, dining room, family room and formal powder room. The main living quarters features five bedrooms, each of which has its own private bath, while a passageway through the dining area leads to the service rooms, which include the kitchen, laundry room and maid's quarters.

"Outside, a circular staircase connects the upper living area terrace to the lower terrace off the entertainment room. An adjoining game room and bathroom are situated under the paved veranda. The defining theme of the landscaping was provided by the small stream that crosses the grounds. The path of the stream was diverted to create two small lakes in the middle of the estate, one of which features a charming waterfall. Accenting the terraces and swimming pool, the hardscape includes a custom bridge over the water plan. The pool, designed in a dramatic movie theatre shape, is lined by Dutch tiles and framed with granite at the edge of the steps."

To contact Ricardo Mayer, call (55) 21-256-8616 or fax (55) 21-256-8616; Ricardo's office is located at 680-708 Avenida Copacabana, Rio de Janeiro, Brazil 22050.

PHOTOGRAPHY: JUCA MORAES

McGEE HOWLE & ASSOCIATES

Vero Beach, Florida

A native of South Carolina, Glenn McGee graduated from Clemson University with a Bachelor of Architecture degree. He is professionally licensed in both architecture and interior design, with memberships in both the American Institute of Architects and the American Society of Interior Designers. Glenn's thirty-year career has spanned seven states and includes travel and study in France, Italy, Switzerland, Austria, Canada, the Bahamas and Saudi Arabia. In addition to his prestigious career as a designer, Mr. McGee has been active as a lecturer on interior design and architectural history at the University of South Carolina.

Also a South Carolina native, Harry Howle is a graduate of the University of Georgia. He is professionally licensed in both architecture and landscape architecture, and maintains memberships in the American Institute of Architects and the American Society of Landscape Architects. Harry has traveled abroad to places such as England, France, Italy and the West Indies to enhance his knowledge and appreciation of varied styles of classical architecture.

Through their diversification of talents and their cohesive flexibility of teamwork, Glenn and Harry are able to offer their clients multi-dimensional services for all facets of design required in achieving a successful project. The firm specializes in custom residential design work.

"Located midway on the eastern coast of Florida is the small township of Indian River Shores. Here you can find the winter residences of many Americans and Europeans in the pristine development of John's Island. The residence shown on this page and the pages that follow represents the work of McGee-Howle and Associates of Vero Beach, Florida. Partners H. Glenn McGee, Architect – Interior Designer, and Harry G. Howle, Architect – Landscape Architect, work closely together to develop all aspects of their designs.

"Our client, a native of Tennessee, requested a relaxed design concept which would reflect his lifestyle. Shown here is the result of blending British Colonial style with a Caribbean Island feeling and the substance of Georgian architecture. This casual approach is enhanced with natural shell stone floors and soft sandy colors. Architectural colors are muted to serve as a neutral background for the large collection of art and antiques brought together by the discerning client. All of these design elements combine to create a sense of place in the beautiful State of Florida."

To contact McGee Howle & Associates Architects, Inc., call (561) 231-4222 or fax (561) 231-4311; Glenn and Harry's office is located at 2801 Ocean Drive, Suite 302, Vero Beach, Florida 32963.

PHOTOGRAPHY: RAYMOND MARTINOT

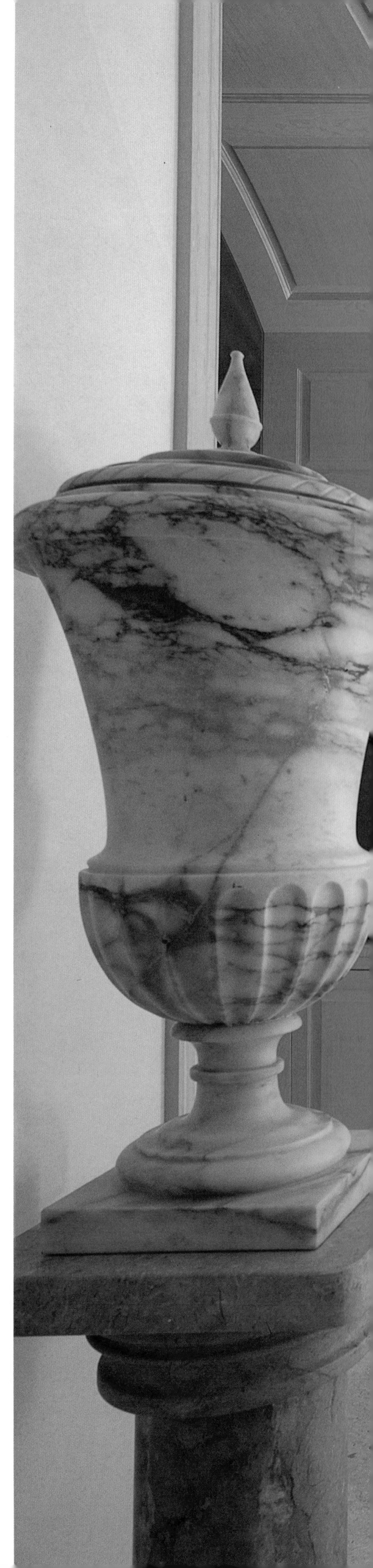

WONDERS
SEA

David Leadbetter's
Faults and Fixes

FRAN MURPHY, ASID, CKD

Saddle River, New Jersey

A Professional Member of the American Society of Interior Designers and a Certified Kitchen Designer, Fran Murphy specializes in residential and executive office design. She has designed residences in New Jersey, New York, Connecticut, Pennsylvania, Florida, California, Mexico, and Paris. Fran is a partner in both D'Image Associates and Details and Design, a gift and accessory shop in Saddle River.

Ms. Murphy is the winner of numerous awards, including several from the National Kitchen & Bath Association, and has participated in many prestigious showhouses in the New York/New Jersey area. A space designed with her partners for the 1994 Mansions in May Showhouse received the "Best Room in Show" award. Her projects have been featured in numerous publications, including *Better Homes & Gardens, Kitchens & Baths, New Jersey Monthly, New Jersey Country Roads, Design New Jersey, The Star Ledger, The Bergen Record, New York Times,* and *Who's Who in Interior Design*. She has also appeared on Good Day New York and Fox Television.

"Every room I design must meet four criteria. First, it must delight the eye, from its initial impact to the gradual unfolding of small, carefully integrated touches. Second, it must be comfortable. Scale and intimacy are important to even the grandest spaces. Third, it must function appropriately, as dictated by the needs of the client. And, fourth, the decor should be timeless. Major pieces should be rooted in traditional styles that transcend cycles of taste. Fads belong in the accessories."

To contact Fran Murphy, call (201) 934-5420 or fax her at (201) 934-5597; Fran's office is located at 71 East Allendale Road, Saddle River, New Jersey 07458.

PHOTOGRAPHY: ROBERT FAULKNER

WAJIH NACCACHE

Dubai, United Arab Emirates

Born in Beirut and fluent in Arabic, French, Italian and English, Wajih Naccache is a designer on a truly international scale. He began his education at the Beaux Arts in Beirut, where he received a Bachelor's degree in Architecture. He continued his studies in Florence at the University Institute Bell Arts, receiving his Master's degree in Interior Design.

After spending several years in Italy to watch, learn, and expand his knowledge, Wajih decided to open his own firm in Dubai, specializing in architectural and interior design. In 1980, the business expanded with the opening of his own furniture showroom. Mr. Naccache relishes working on the whole project, an entire house or estate, where he can create a total environment befitting each client's personality and taste. He has devoted more than twenty years to creating luxurious residences, palaces, and hotels for numerous clients throughout the Middle East, Europe and other areas of the world. Most recently, he completed several royal and presidential suites for the Crown Plaza Hotel in Dubai.

"In this lavish Dubai villa belonging to a businessman with a cosmopolitan and highly cultivated lifestyle, I designed a polished interior with simplified lines to focus attention on the European antiques. The neoclassical design of the double volume entrance hall sets the stage for a grand reception and leads to the main wings of the villa and the gardens outside. The circa 1820 marble urns are Italian.

"The living room, which looks into the garden through a big bay window, was divided into two levels and creates two different living spaces. I felt this would contribute to the villa's open feeling. A magnificent Italian Orientalist painting is the main focal point of the room and provides a rich background for the sofa, which was lined with a large striped fabric. Two white marble pedestals and vases frame this elegant setting."

To contact Wajih Naccache, call (971) 6-593-035 or fax (971) 6-597-521; Post Office Box 1776, Sharjah, U.A.E. Wajih's Showroom is located in Dubai, telephone (971) 4-826-767.

PREM NATH, FIIA, ASID, FIID

Bombay, India

A professional interior designer and architect, Prem Nath is based in Bombay and has been in practice since 1965. His firm, Prem Nath & Associates, is a total design and consulting organization which handles architectural interior design, including engineering services for residential, commercial, corporate, hotel, resort and institutional works. A branch office in Delhi also handles architecture and interior designing services, as well as project management consultancy services. Mr. Nath was born in 1941, and graduated from Bombay's Sir J.J. College of Architecture in 1965. He has handled many prestigious assignments, including the interiors of the homes of celebrities and film stars, the Art Today Art Gallery, the Vasant Valley School in Delhi, the ISKON Temple, and numerous Citibank offices. Mr. Nath is currently president of the Indian Institute of Interior Designers.

"In the traditional or religious Indian home, a small entrance lobby is often decorated with a picture or deity of their god or goddess for salutation every time one enters or leaves the home. In the photo featured on the opposite page, the deity is portrayed in graphic form – hand etched and engraved in the mirror with colors of jewels and ornamentation. This subtle dedication blends with the stone bracket and shelf, decorated with a small pot in which offerings of flowers have been placed. The planters and a chair complete the setting for the small entrance/foyer. In this same apartment, belonging to a young Indian couple, a large circular and revolving bed is the focal point of the romantic bedroom pictured below. The wall canopy is adorned in tie-dye silk flairs and trimmed with braids and tassels.

"The following page shows the overall simple decor of the dining room. The intricate design of the wooden handcrafted chairs, finished with *faux* marbling, contributes as the main decor feature. The use of mirrors in the corridor and adjoining small living room gives these two areas a more spacious look. The decor is a blend of modern and traditional fittings which brings a feeling of drama into an otherwise routine interior. All handmade, hand etched stained glass door panels or shutters decorate the dining room. This room was designed to be an extension of the lobby and living room areas. Simply designed chairs and the use of a glass top dining table offset the decorative surroundings and enhance the ambience."

To contact Prem Nath, call (91) 22-202-0029, 22-202-0786, or fax (91) 22-287-5150; Prem's office is located at 4 Merewether Road, Bombay 400 001, India.

AHMED NOUR

Cairo, Egypt

Egyptian architect Ahmed Nour completed his B.Sc. in Architecture from the Faculty of Fine Arts in Cairo in 1965. He began his career in Kuwait, then, in 1977, expanded his business, ASA Consultants, to his hometown of Cairo. Mr. Nour has designed residential projects, offices, shopping malls, hotels, sea and desert resorts, and recreational projects throughout the Gulf area and in Egypt. He brings to each project his expertise in architecture and guidance in interiors and landscaping. In addition to the Hurghada Marriott Hotel featured here, other recent projects by ASA Consultants include Park Plaza Hurghada Resort, Sheraton Sharm El Sheikh Mountain Hotel, Kuwait Airways Headquarters, and the Cairo Aqua Park.

"The most elegant Red Sea five-star hotel, the Hurghada Marriott, has three hundred rooms situated on five typical floors, all of which enjoy the spectacular sea view and surround the main hotel patio and distinctively-shaped swimming pool. The hotel's entrance is modern, but with a pharaonic touch, and gives way to areas which include the reception and information counter, lift cores, main restaurant, main patio, lounge, bar, shopping arcade, swimming pool and beach. Each of these components of the hotel was designed so that an excellent sea view could be experienced from any room in which one might be settled.

"A diving center was constructed of wood, a marina accommodates full facilities, and a large island is connected to the hotel beach via an attractive wooden bridge. The hotel's specialty restaurant sits in a quiet corner facing the sea. Guests also have access to a wide variety of amenities such as a large health club, squash courts, and tennis courts. Every feature of the hotel was designed to be harmonious, and yet each is different from the next."

To contact Ahmed Nour, call ASA Consultants at (20) 2-262-7877, 2-262-9664, 2-261-0540 or fax (20) 2-262-4163; Ahmed's office is located at 8 Sebawieh Al-Masry Street, Nasser City, Cairo, Egypt.

FERESHTEH B. NYBE

London, England

Fereshteh Nybe was educated at the University of North Carolina and received her Bachelor of Creative Arts degree in 1985. She was awarded a commendation for outstanding scholarship student while obtaining her Master's degree and her love for learning has led Fereshteh to teach others at the nearby university. Ms. Nybe has traveled extensively throughout Europe and Asia, studying the designs of other countries and cultures in order to better serve her diverse clientele.

In 1988, Ms. Nybe established her own design firm where she is owner and principal designer. Working with different clients whose needs and styles vary greatly, Fereshteh specializes in residential and commercial design and has done numerous projects which include the interior and exterior design of many private residences and public buildings. A serious hobbyist in the translation of psychology books, Fereshteh believes that this knowledge gives her a better understanding and increased ability to communicate her clients' lifestyles, feelings, and personalities through her design. This coincides with her philosophy that, in order to have happy and satisfied clients, you need to recognize their uniqueness. Her belief is that design is a reflection of life.

With a great interest in antiques and a passion for traditional and aged materials, Ms. Nybe is able to blend Oriental and classical designs together successfully.

"In this large private residence, the centerpoint of the living room is dominated by a magnificent handmade copper fireplace. The wood floor has been stained a warm honey color and displays the beautiful Persian rugs, which in turn become the base for the elegant handmade Jacob's French design furniture in antique gold. The surrounding walls are mirrored, as are the two columns and archway dividing the living and dining rooms. There are two large, round chandeliers with crystal baubles in this area – one of which hangs low above the dining room table and reflects onto the antique crystal candlesticks placed atop the table.

"Other pieces featured in this room include gold buffets and a fabulous round service table which divides the living room area. Many fine handmade sterling silver pieces accessorize tabletops and buffets, while warm and dramatic colors were used to lend an inviting, cozy look to the elegance of the rooms."

JON OSMAN, RIBA

Roadtown Tortola, British Virgin Islands

British-born Jon Osman has resided in the British Virgin Islands for twenty-four years. Living in a tranquil, yet sometimes harsh climate, his philosophy is to create architecture that will harmonize with nature – to blend with and enhance the surroundings and to create human environments that are peaceful and conducive to fulfilling the spirit and ambience of these tropical islands, as well as satisfying his personal qualifications of successful architecture, functionality, cost effectiveness and creativity.

"The main house of this private retreat on Necker Island in the British Virgin Islands is designed to bring the exotic flavor of Indonesia to the Caribbean. The buildings are constructed of sturdy local field stone columns and the roofs are made of huge hardwood timbers from the Brazilian jungle. Adaptable to withstand the harsh tropical climate, the buildings can be closed up with solid hardwood shutters or left completely open, as can be seen by the retractable roof openings that permit sunlight to flood into the central planter in the sitting room. Arranged with a selection of Indonesian furnishings and adorned with the vibrant batik and ikat fabrics for which Bali is renowned, the atmosphere is one of casual elegance. The highest spot on the island is the master bedroom with truly spectacular views out across the confluence of the Atlantic and the Caribbean. Rising from the turquoise seas, encircled by majestic coral reefs and pristine sandy beaches, the island is topped by the 22,000 square foot retreat, designed to form a natural continuation of the hilltop. The openness of internal design and embellishment of furnishings and decoration are conceived to evoke both the essence of a Balinese ambience and a place to be at peace.

"Little Thatch Island, featured below, is a South Pacific-styled private residence with 10,000 square feet of, appropriately, thatched roof buildings – a main house with spacious terraces designed to accommodate twenty guests, a walk-in swimming pool that visually vanishes into the Caribbean Sea and five separate bedroom villas are set in tropical gardens."

To contact Jon Osman, call (809) 494-2343, fax (809) 494-5956, or e-mail osman@caribsurf.com; Jon's office is located Box 833, Roadtown Tortola, British Virgin Islands.

PHOTOGRAPHY: DOUGAL D. THORNTON

CORAL REEFS

JOSHUA JIH PAN, FAIA

Taipei, Taiwan

Joshua Pan founded J.J. Pan and Partners, an architectural and planning firm, in 1981. Dedicated to providing creative solutions in the design and planning of human environments, the company combines a proven track record, advanced education, talented design capability, diversified technical experience, and a wide range of professional, teaching, and research backgrounds into a world-class service package for clients in Taiwan and around the globe. J.J. Pan and Partners has consistently provided top quality services, and their clients have come to expect the highest levels of professional expertise in handling complex large-scale projects. Such accomplishment is also reflected in the numerous awards for design excellence the firm has received. In 1994, in recognition of a career of distinction, Mr. Pan was elected a Fellow by the AIA. Completed projects include residential communities, college campuses, industrial parks, research laboratories, educational and medical facilities, and landscape and interior design.

"The rectalinear, high-tech factory headquarters building shown below and to the right has a five meter drop in longitudinal direction. The design places the entrance to underground parking at the lower end, while the service/loading area is at the higher side on the opposite end, thus freeing a commanding view of a park across the way. The following photographs are another high-tech facility in Taiwan. The exterior is metal curtainwall with four tones of gray and strong accent-colored window frames to convey a state-of-the-art image. A series of vertical transportation cores and shafts were introduced to this exterior design, breaking down the overpowering volume and creating rhythm within the complex. The next project shown is the renovation of a private residence. Simplicity and light colors are emphasized to create an airy atmosphere. Lastly, a rhythmic saw-tooth building facade is instrumental in reducing the scale of this building which houses a gymnasium and Olympic-size indoor pool, and leads the way to the athletic field beyond."

To contact Joshua Pan, call (886) 2-701-2617 or fax (886) 2-700-4489; Joshua's office is located at 21, Alley 12, Lane 118, Ren Ai Road, Sec. 3, Taipei, Taiwan.

EILEEN PERETZ

New York, New York

With a primary office in New York and an office in Paris, Eileen Peretz Interiors' projects span the continents while their styles draw upon the best of the present and the past. An expert in 19th and 20th century antiques and fine art, Ms. Peretz is equally acclaimed for her original furniture designs. Her approach to a project begins with interviews designed to encourage the client to become more aware of his or her tastes, lifestyle and special needs. She views the client/designer relationship as a unique collaboration, offering the designer an opportunity to introduce the client to the world of interior design, fine art and antiques. Ms. Peretz is, herself, an avid collector whose personal collection includes works by Picasso, Matisse and Archipenko as well as Anselm Kiefer and Sol Lewitt. In Paris, she collects art deco furniture and *objets d'art*. With thirty years in the field of interior design in her background, Eileen approaches her work with continued enthusiasm and the benefits of experience and innovation.

Trained in sculpture, fine arts, art history and architectural design, Ms. Peretz earned a Bachelor of Fine Arts degree before continuing her studies and certification in interior design. Ms. Peretz has written an interior design column for a New York newspaper and has taught and lectured extensively on interior design and space planning. She is an Associate Member of the American Society of Interior Designers. Ms. Peretz has been named in *Who's Who in International Interior Design, Who's Who in America* and *Who's Who in the East.*

"This home was designed for a young family. It presented a particularly exciting challenge. My clients wanted their living room to express a combination of warmth and casual elegance. I suggested a fairly soft palette of cremes and yellows, accented by touches of black to visually enlarge the space. The clients were enthusiastic about the choice. The seating is comfortable and inviting. Lush window treatments add an illusion of height to the contemporary architecture of the room. I designed the lamp tables to complement the Biedermeier secretary seen reflected in the framed mirror above the sofa. The use of antique Biedermeier is a distinguishing element in the room. Its rich color gives the room a touch of formality while its classic lines reflect timelessnes.

"We then decided to give the dining room a more formal look. A Chinese needlepoint rug was chosen to define the space. The deep colors of this exquisite rug are seen in the reflections of the mirrored wainscoting around the room. The yellow gold of the walls and the aubergines in the fabrics complement the colors in the rug perfectly and give the room a peaceful glow. Warm woods and the use of bold, luxurious colors and textures create a pleasing atmosphere for evening entertainment."

To contact Eileen Peretz, call (212) 873-1307; Eileen's office is located at 300 Central Park West, New York, New York 10024. To contact the Paris office, call 1-45-44-82-44; it is located at 32, Rue de Varenne, 75007 Paris.

PHOTOGRAPHY: TERRENCE MICHAEL TIERNEY

LASTING IMPRESSIONS
100 DESIGNERS' FAVORITE ROOMS
Biedermeier

FRANK S. PERRY, IIDA

Chicago, Illinois

Frank S. Perry Residential Interiors Inc. offers a full range of professional services incorporating interior design, architectural services, and construction management. The firm was established in 1982 by Frank Perry, a Chicago native and member of IIDA.

©Traditional Home Magazine, Meredith Corporation, 1993

Mr. Perry is noted for his ability to balance both antiques with soft contemporary furnishings to create a look that personifies classical luxury. His design repertoire embodies a wide range of styles – from elegant, urbane city dwellings to relaxed, gracious country homes. Every Perry design incorporates rich furnishings, lush textures and warm colors to create dramatic interiors. For each project, Mr. Perry strategically focuses on integrating the architecture and the lifestyles of his clients into the details of his projects. The final results are designs of quality, comfort, and uniqueness. His hallmark is being especially attentive to his clients – from the inception to completion of the project. "Within this framework, I can also concentrate on providing the exquisite details that my clients and I demand." Favorite projects are often those that, when finished, have created not only beautiful rooms, but a lasting friendship.

"When my clients and I met, they had been living in this vintage co-op in Chicago's Gold Coast for several years and were ready for a dramatic design change. They had acquired a taste for the styles of Northern Italy during a recent trip to that region. Once the theme was chosen, the living room and library became our priorities. With dark oak as the predominant motif, the living room's plaster beams were transformed through *faux* painting. An antique marble mantlepiece replaced the old, and the original hardwood floors were refinished with a dark oak stain. In the library, cast plaster crown and ceiling moldings were added. French doors with beveled glass panes and a built-in media cabinet became our finishing touch. The client's well chosen accessories, such as the Chinese roof tile mounted on a mahogany stand, richly colored tapestries, and fabrics of plush velvets and woven brocades in golds, greens, and burgundies, harmonize warmly to create the regional integrity of Northern Italy right in the heart of Chicago."

To contact Frank S. Perry, call (312) 280-0850 or fax (312) 280-8978; Frank's office is located at 180 East Pearson Street, Suite 5102, Chicago, Illinois 60611.

PHOTOGRAPHY: SCOTT MCDONALD

GERD RAMSTAD

Jar, Norway

In her native Norway, Gerd Ramstad is a commercial and residential interior designer and architect. A graduate of Bergen University, Ms. Ramstad has won numerous international awards for contract interior design, as well as finalist awards for her furniture designs. Her work has been exhibited in Helsinki's Habitare and the Museum of Modern Art in Tokyo, Japan. Based in Jar, near Oslo, Ms. Ramstad focuses on shops, schools, hotels and hospitals. Her major projects include interior design work for the University Kristiansand, the Klekken Hotel, and the main offices of Norway's Nordberg Group. As an exciting addition to Ms. Ramstad's past work, she was given the opportunity to take part in the 1994 Olympics at Lillehammer, designing VIP rooms and executive centers. In the same year, she also had the pleasure of decorating the first Hospice in Norway.

"The project shown on this page is the University of Agder in Kristiansand, South Norway, which was converted from a hospital space to a school campus. Chairs were specially designed by this designer, and a collection of beat art from San Francisco decorate several walls of buildings throughout the university. The counter in the students' reception and general office area is made entirely of aspen wood.

"The Norwegian Railways main information center at Lillehammer featured on the following pages reflects a work-friendly atmosphere among the data operators at their PC work stations. We framed the stations with specially composed textiles and covered the terminal desks with a sound suppressing fabric to minimize interference between the operators. Special cable trunks conceal the typical 'bird's nest' of wires and cables between each of the data units. We also transformed the employee lunchroom. Expressly designed chairs from Ramstad Arkitekt/Design received a prestigious quality design award in 1996."

To contact Gerd Ramstad, call (47) 67-53-04-58 or fax (47) 67-12-34-10; Gerd's office is located at Lovenskioldsvei 16-B, 1342 Jar, Norway.

PHOTOGRAPHY: SIGBJORN LENESE REKLAMEFOTO A/S

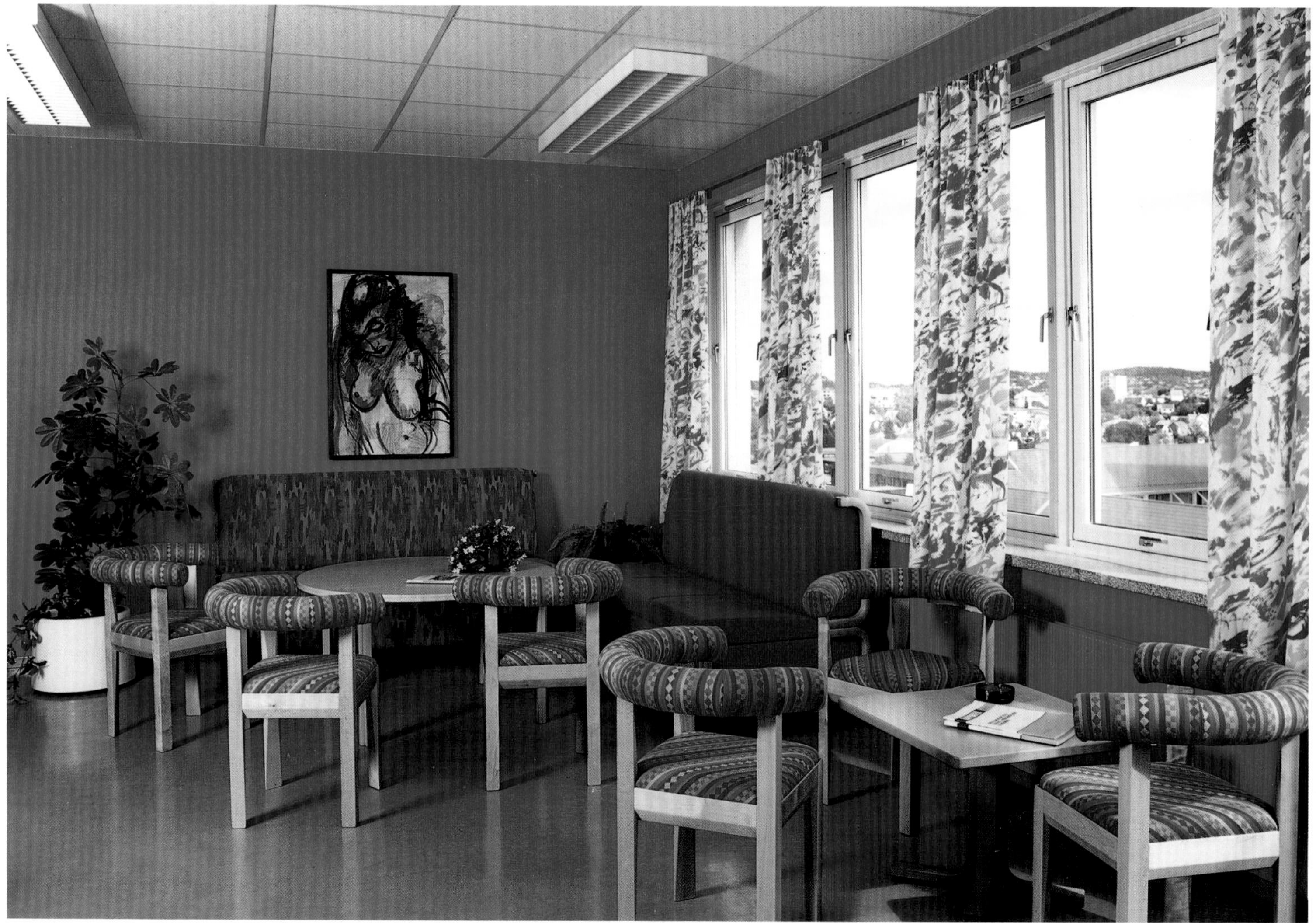

WORLDWIDE DESIGNS BY IBJ

Pound, Wisconsin

With over 30 years of buying and designing expertise, both here in the United States and abroad, Jaci Yoap offers her clients a continually expanding knowledge and unique inventory of fine furniture and works of art. She has acquired a vast collection of exquisite European and Victorian antiques, selected furniture, and Oriental *objets d'art*.

In addition to her own diverse projects, which include interior design and the manufacture and marketing of her own exclusive line of furnishings, Jaci works skillfully with other designers, supplying them from her inventory and exposing them to her vast array of resources. A specialist in blending Oriental, Victorian and French designs, Ms. Yoap lectures on various design topics, antiques, and the arts and customs of the Chinese culture.

"A palette of soft colors enhances the softness and warmth of the large tower office featured below. We combined fine Italian and French antiques to replace the usual office furnishings. A mixture of bronzes, intricately carved cherubs, fine porcelain, and silk-wrapped roses entwining the silk *moire* drapery all add to the luxury of this office. On the opposite page, natural daylight enlivens the details of the fine carvings of this office furnished in rosewood. Settings for the offices and conference room in the background have been created for the play of antiques, collections and other personal treasures."

To contact Jaci Yoap, call (920) 897-3536 or fax (920) 897-2825; Jaci's office is located at W6748 County Road B, Pound, Wisconsin 54161, e-mail: jaciy@juno.com.

PHOTOGRAPHY: VAL IHDE

DANISH A. ZUBY, MCSD

Karachi, Pakistan

Danish Zuby is a leading interior design professional in Pakistan and has been practicing in Karachi for the past fifteen years. On his return from England in 1980, where he received his formal interior design education, he worked on the Karachi Sheraton Hotel project before joining ASA, a leading architectural firm. Mr. Zuby was head of ASA's interior design department until 1989, at which time he founded his own practice in a small design studio on Shaheed-e-Millat Road in Karachi. His firm has grown to become one of the most sought-after design shops in the region. Mr. Zuby's clients include the Karachi Sheraton, Holiday Inn, Glaxo, Pizza Hut, Jardine Fleming, Crosby Securities, BASF and the 3M Corporation. The photos in this presentation are of three restaurants designed for Holiday Inn Crowne Plaza and, on the following two pages, the Pakistani Restaurant at the Karachi Sheraton.

"The interior ambiance of the Pakistani Restaurant at the Sheraton Hotel in Karachi was envisioned to become a catalyst and initiator for an Arts and Crafts movement in the

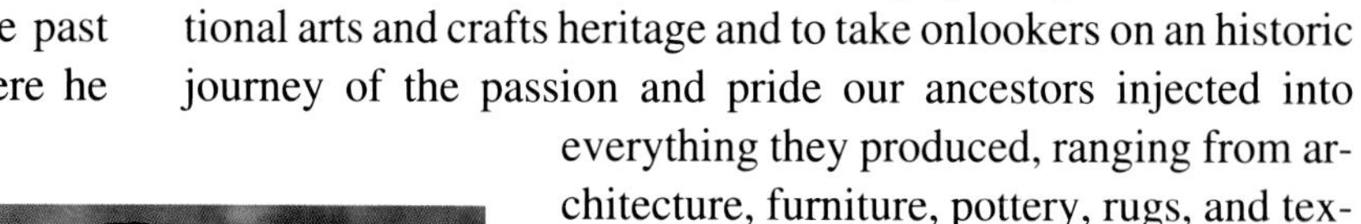

country I cherish. The idea was to display images of our traditional arts and crafts heritage and to take onlookers on an historic journey of the passion and pride our ancestors injected into everything they produced, ranging from architecture, furniture, pottery, rugs, and textiles. Our intent is to inspire the desire to bring back the quality of skills, trades and professions we once mastered in this labor-rich country.

"We accomplished this goal by giving credence to each of our four provinces, with special attention to costumes, music, dance and, of course, their cuisine. All waiters wear regional dress, while the walls are adorned with traditional relics. A large earthen Tandoor is visible through the glazed counter to allow guests a view of the traditional way of preparing bread 'Naans'."

To contact Danish Zuby, call (92) 21-455-7129 or fax (92) 21-455-8339; Danish's office is located at Samar Heights, Ground Floor, S2, 1/4 DMCHS, Shaheed-e-Millat Road, Karachi 74800, Pakistan.

Indexes . . .

INDEXES

Designers Index: Whether for a private residence or for a commercial project, selecting the right architect or interior designer is rarely an easy choice. To assist you with your decision, this book has been specially edited to act as a portfolio illustrating the finest work of a wide range of the world's leading architects and interior designers.

On the preceding pages, you have had the opportunity to see each designer and to learn about their backgrounds and qualifications. You have been able to see their best design projects and read each designer's explanation of how they rose to the challenges each project presented. If this book has been successful, you probably have at least one designer or architect in mind to interview for your upcoming project. After selecting a designer offering the right style, the right look, and the right design philosophy, the next question usually concerns fees and payment structures.

On the following pages, each of the participating designers and architects have provided contact information, a listing of their design specializations, and a general idea of their design fees. Almost all of the designers and architects featured in this edition work internationally, and all have agreed to provide immediate attention to inquiries from readers of this book.

Photographers Index: For the professional designer or architect, this book doubles as an international portfolio of the world's best interior and architectural photographers. The preceding pages have featured the finest examples of their work, and you are now invited to use the following index to locate and contact these professionals for projects throughout the world. Each index listing includes the photographer's name, company, address, telephone and fax numbers, as well as the pages on which their work appears. Whether your projects are in North America, Asia, South America, Europe or the Middle East, this index is a convenient contact directory of qualified interior and architectural photographers virtually anywhere in the world.

Designers Index

Adams Design, Inc.
Jack Adams, ASID
1415 Kalakaua Avenue, Ste. 204
Honolulu, HI 96826
Tel.: (808) 955-6100, Fax: (808) 947-4311
Residential, office, contract, hotel and restaurant interior design.
Fee structure: varies according to project
Pages: 10-11

Ahara Prima Design PT
Gaby Widajanti, HDII
Times Square Building, Suite 8D,
Jl. H.R. Rasuna Said Blok X-1
Kav. 1 & 2, Kuningan, Jakarta, Indonesia 12950
Tel.: (62) 21-526-1370, Fax: (62) 21-526-1470
Office, retail, hotel and restaurant interior design.
Fee structure: varies according to project; negotiable.
Pages: 12-13

Rashid Saad Al-Rashid
Rashid Saad Al-Rashid, Architect
Al-Rashid Center
Post Office Box 16557
Riyadh 11474, Saudi Arabia
Tel.: (966) 1-465-6796, 404-4376,
Fax: (966) 1-403-0521
Residential, regional shopping mall, community facility, hotel, restaurant and office building architectural and interior design.
Fee structure: varies according to project.
Pages: 14-19

Fahad M. Al-Solaiman
Saudi Arabia Standards Org.
P.O. Box 26828
Riyadh 11496, Saudi Arabia
Tel.: (966) 1-476-5893, Fax: (966) 1-479-0581
Residential, office, hotel and restaurant interior design.
Fee structure: varies according to project.
Pages: 20-25

Lucille Anderson, Allied ASID
Works of Wonder
265 North Main Street
Munroe Falls, OH 44262
Tel.: (330) 688-0969, Fax: (330) 688-0155
Residential, commercial and senior living facility interior design.
Fee structure: consulting fee; retail.
Pages: 26-27

Anthony Antine
Antine Associates
200 East 77th Street
New York, NY 10021
Tel.: (212) 988-4096

1028 Aracadian Way
Palisade, NJ 07024
Tel.: (201) 224-0315, Fax: (201) 224-5963
Residential, hotel and restaurant interior design.
Fee structure: design fee plus percentage.
Pages: 28-31

Samir Badro
Green Line Company, Ltd.
Box 5835
Sharjah, United Arab Emirates
Tel.: (971) 6-333-731, Fax: (971) 6-332-650

Green Line Company
P.O. Box 9227
Dubai, United Arab Emirates
Tel.: (971) 4-313-563, Fax: (971) 4-310-574

Green Line Company
Sheikh Suroor Bin Mohammad Al Nahyan Building
Corniche Road
Abu Dhabi, United Arab Emirates
Tel.: (971) 2-656-533, Fax: (971) 2-656-662

G.L. Interiors, W.L.L.
Tayar Center, P.O. Box 55066
Sin El Fil, Beirut, Lebanon
Tel.: (961) 1-500-866, Fax: (961) 1-492-599

G.L. Syria Ltd.
Al Abbaseen Square, Bshara Al Khoury Street
P.O. Box 7615
Damascus, Syria
Tel.: (963) 11-334-162, Fax: (963) 11-247-780

Green Line Inc. (Le Coin)
115 South Robertson Boulevard
Los Angeles, California 90048, USA
Tel.: (310) 274-8413, Fax: (310) 247-1601

GLM Corporation
7360 SW 116th Terrace
Miami, FL 33156
Tel.: (305) 858-8080, Fax: (305) 854-6064

G.L. Company Ltd.
14 Craufurd Rise, Maidenhead, Berkshire
London SL6 7LX, United Kingdom
Tel.: (44) 1628-26333, Fax: (44) 1628-770340

G.L. Co. France
6, Rue du Mont Thabor
Paris 75001, France
Tel.: (33) 1-42-61-76-16, Fax: (33) 1-42-86-87-97

G.L. Co.
Via Meichiorre, Gioia 41
Milano, Italy
Tel.: (39) 2-66-98-42-01, Fax: (39) 2-67-00-482

Residential and commercial architectural and interior design.
Fee structure: available upon request.
Pages 32-33

Viorica Belcic
V-3 Design
50 West 96th Street
New York, NY 10025
Tel.: (212) 222-2551, Fax: (212) 222-2201
Residential interior design.
Fee structure: available upon request
Pages: 34-37

Dorothy Bocchino, Allied ASID
D'Image Associates
71 East Allendale Road
Saddle River, NJ 07458
Tel.: (201) 934-5420, Fax: (201) 934-5597
Residential interior design.
Fee structure: available upon request.
Pages: 38-39

Anita Brooks
Anita Brooks Interior Design
4270 S. Cameron, Suite 1
Las Vegas, NV 89103
Tel.: (702) 364-5888, Fax: (702) 364-0503
Residential and hospitality interior design.
Fee structure: varies according to project.
Pages: 40-41

Michael de Santis, ASID
Michael de Santis, Inc.
1110 Second Avenue
New York, New York 10022
Tel.: (212) 753-8871, Fax: (212) 935-7777
Residential interior design.
Fee structure: varies according to project.
Pages: 42-47

Suellen DeFrancis, IIDA
900 Park Avenue
New York, New York 10021
Tel.: (212) 879-8386, Fax: (212) 879-3136
Residential, office, contract, hotel and restaurant interior design.
Fee structure: varies according to project
Pages: 48-49

Diwan Interiors International
Iman D. Harby & Fouad Nassar
Post Office Box 2071
Salmiah 22021, Kuwait
Tel.: (965) 574-8765, Fax: (965) 574-8760
Residential, office, contract, hotel and restaurant architectural design and interior contracting.
Fee structure: varies according to project.
Pages: 50-55

Lovejoy Duryea, ASID, IIDA, IDEC
Dorset Design Inc.
372 Fifth Avenue, Suite 8F
New York, NY 10018
Tel.: (212) 290-2299, Fax: (212) 714-1943

c/o School of Visual Arts
209 East 23rd Street
New York, NY 10018
Tel.: (212) 592-2572, Fax: (212) 592-2573
E-mail: ldureya@adm.schoolofvisualarts.edu
Residential interior design.
Fee structure: hourly or percentage of construction, depending upon project details.
Pages: 56-57

William R. Eubanks
William R. Eubanks Interior Design, Inc.
1516 Union Avenue
Memphis, TN 38104
Tel.: (901) 272-1825, Fax: (901) 272-1845
Residential and office interior design.
Fee structure: varies according to project.
Pages: 58-61

Naglaa A. Farsi
Rue des Creusets 32
Sion 1950, Switzerland
Tel.: (41) 27-323-4225, Fax: (41) 27-323-4226
Residential, office, contract, hotel and restaurant interior design.
Fee structure: varies according to project
Pages: 62-63

Laura Goomas, Allied ASID
D'Image Associates
71 East Allendale Road
Saddle River, NJ 07458
Tel.: (201) 934-5420, Fax: (201) 934-5597
Residential and contract interior design.
Fee structure: available upon request.
Pages: 64-65

Amr. Ahmed Hafez
Ahmed Hafez & Company
5 El Kes Abadeer Roushdy
Alexandria, Egypt
Tel.: (20) 3-848-884, Fax: (20) 3-586-8710
Residential, office, contract, hotel and restaurant interior design.
Fee structure: varies according to project.
Pages: 66-67

Constance W. Hummel, IIDA
Winston-Scott Interiors
425 White Oak Lane
Barrington, IL 60010
Tel.: (847) 304-1010, Fax: (847) 304-1040
Residential, office, and contract interior design.
Fee structure: available upon request.
Pages: 68-69

Frederic Jochem
Frederic Jochem Architectural Interiors
240 Central Park South
New York, NY 10019
Tel.: (212) 956-1840, Fax: (212) 956-1845
Residential, contract, showroom, lobby and gallery interior design.
Fee structure: available upon request.
Pages: 70-73, 170

Peter Jöhnk
Peter Jöhnk Innearchitekt
Wandsbeker Konigstrasse 50
22041 Hamburg, Germany
Tel.: (49) 40-689421-0, Fax: (49) 40-689421-30
Residential, office, contract, hotel and restaurant interior design.
Fee structure: varies according to project.
Pages: 74-79

Chip Johnston, ASID, IFDA
2996 Grandview Avenue NE
Suite 300
Atlanta, GA 30305-3245
Tel.: (404) 231-4141, Fax: (404) 261-3713
Residential and office interior design.
Fee structure: available upon request.
Pages: 80-83

Judith Sisler Johnston, ASID
Sisler Williams Interior Design
9143 Phillips Hwy.
Jacksonville, FL 32256
Tel.: (904) 363-0177, Fax: (904) 363-9980
Residential, model home and retirement community interior design.
Fee structure: varies according to project.
Pages: 84-89

Payal Kapoor
Visions Interior Designers & Consultants
A-1/140, Safdarjung Enclave
New Delhi 110 029, India
Tel.: (91) 11-619-6115, 610-7522,
Fax: (91) 11-619-3570
Residential, office, contract, hotel, restaurant, school and institutional interior design.
Fee structure: varies according to project.
Pages: 90-91

Nancy Kwok, MCSD
Hinex Universal Design Consultants Co. Ltd.
Room 1302, Wealthy Industrial Building
22-26 Wing Yip Street
Kwai Chung, Hong Kong
Tel.: (852) 2-589-0700, Fax: (852) 2-589-0708
Residential, office, hotel and restaurant interior design.
Fee structure: percentage.
Pages: 92-95

La Maison Fleurie, Inc.
Annick Presles
Paramount, 139 Country Rd., Ste. 20A
Palm Beach, FL 33480
Tel.: (561) 833-1083, Fax: (561) 833-9318
Residential, office, contract, hotel and restaurant interior design.
Fee structure: varies according to project.
Pages: 96-99

Donald W. Lilly, ASID
Donald Lilly Associates Interior Design, Inc.
River Plaza
900 S. U.S. Highway One, Suite 303
Jupiter, FL 33477
Tel.: (561) 746-5010, Fax: (561) 743-4398

Donald Lilly Associates Interior Design, Inc.
Ocean Reef Club, 100 Anchor Drive, Suite 400
Key Largo, FL 33037
Tel.: (305) 367-4888, Fax: (305) 367-2817

Donald Lilly Associates Interior Design, Inc.
7241 Southwest 168th Street, Suite C
Miami, FL 33157
Tel.: (305) 253-0550, Fax: (305) 253-2552
Residential, contract, hotel, restaurant, nautical and resort interior design.
Fee structure: varies according to project.
Front cover, front flyleaf, pages 1, 3, 7, 9, 100-107, back cover

Ricardo Mayer, ASID, AIA
Av. Copacabana 680-708
Rio de Janeiro 22050, Brazil
Tel.: (55) 21-274-3280, Fax: (55) 21-256-8616
Residential and office interior design.
Fee structure: varies according to project.
Pages: 108-111

McGee Howle & Associates
Glenn McGee, AIA, ASID
2801 Ocean Drive, Ste. 302
Vero Beach, FL 32963
Tel.: (561) 231-4222, Fax: (561) 231-4311
Residential, office, contract, hotel and restaurant interior design.
Fee structure: varies according to project.
Pages: 112-119

Fran Murphy, ASID, CKD
D'Image Associates
71 East Allendale Road
Saddle River, NJ 07458
Tel.: (201) 934-5420, Fax: (201) 934-5597
Residential, office, contract, hotel and restaurant interior design.
Fee structure: varies according to project.
Pages: 120-121

Wajih Naccache
Design Team
Naser Street, P.O. Box 1776
Sharjah, United Arab Emirates
Tel.: (971) 6-593-035, Fax: (971) 6-597-521
Residential, office, contract, hotel and restaurant interior design.
Fee structure: varies according to project.
Pages: 122-125

Prem Nath, FIIA, ASID, FIID
Prem Nath & Associates
Devidas Mansion, First Floor
4, Merewether Road, Apollo Bunder
Bombay 400 039, India
Tel.: (91) 22-202-0029, (91) 22-202-0786,
Fax: (91) 22-287-5150
Residential, office, contract, hotel and restaurant interior design.
Fee structure: varies according to project.
Pages: 126-129

Ahmed Nour
ASA Consultants
8 Sebaway El Masry St.
Cairo, Egypt
Tel.: (20) 2-262-7877, Fax: (20) 2-262-4163
Residential, office, contract, hotel and restaurant interior design.
Fee structure: varies according to project.
Pages: 130-139

Jon Osman, RIBA
Osman, Adams & Partners, Architects
P.O. Box 833, Roadtown
Tortola, British Virgin Islands
Tel.: (809) 494-2343, Fax: (809) 494-5956
E-mail: osman@caribsurf.com
Residential, commercial, hotel and resort, interior design, island development.
Fee structure: varies according to project.
Pages: 140-145

Joshua Jih Pan, FAIA
J.J. Pan & Partners
21, Alley 2, Lane 118, Ren Ai Road, Sec. 3
Taipei, Taiwan
Tel.: (886) 2-701-2617, Fax: (886) 2-700-4489
Residential, office, contract, hotel and restaurant interior design.
Fee structure: varies according to project.
Pages: 146-151

Eileen Peretz, ASID Associate
Eileen Peretz Interiors, Inc.
300 Central Park West
New York, NY 10024
Tel.: (212) 873-8191, Fax: (212) 873-1307

32 Rue de Varenne
75007 Paris, France
Tel.: (44) 1-45-44-82-44
Residential and office interior design.
Fee structure: initial consultation fee, net plus 25%.
Pages: 152-155

Frank S. Perry, IIDA
Frank Perry Residential Interiors, Inc.
180 E. Pearson Street
Chicago, IL 60611
Tel.: (312) 280-0850, Fax: (312) 280-8978
Residential and office interior design.
Fee structure: available upon request.
Pages: 156-157

Gerd Ramstad
Skogvn. 16
1342 Jar, Norway
Tel. (47) 67-53-04-58, Fax: (47) 67-12-34-10
Office, school, hospital, hotel and restaurant interior design.
Fee structure: varies according to project.
Pages: 158-163

Worldwide Designs by IBJ
Jacquelyne Yoap, IFDA
West 6748 Highway B
Pound, WI 54161
Tel.: (920) 897-3536, Fax: (920) 897-2825
E-mail: jaciy@juno.com
Office, retail and showroom interior design.
Fee structure: varies according to project.
Pages: 164-165

Danish A. Zuby, MCSD
DAZ Interiors
Samar Heights, 1/4 DMCHS, Shaheed-e-Millat Road
Karachi 74800, Pakistan
Tel.: (92) 21-455-7129, Fax: (92) 21-455-8339, 263-5277
Residential, office, contract, hotel and restaurant interior design.
Fee structure: available upon request.
Pages: 166-169

Photographers Index

We have endeavored to assure the accuracy of the information provided in these indexes. We welcome information on any oversight, which will be corrected in subsequent printings.